Worship in Heaven

and why on earth it matters

by Tom Kraeuter

Training Resources, Inc., Hillsboro MO

65 Shepherds Way
Hillsboro, MO 63050
636-789-4522
www.training-resources.org

ISBN: 978-1-62486-015-7

Dedication

I humbly dedicate this book to my fellow worship leaders, who, for many years, have focused the attention of our congregation on the One Who reigns forever.

Dave Lorenz

Mary Mahder

Dan Kennedy

Thank you for your selfless ministry and for consistently pointing me—and all of us—to the Lamb on the throne.

Thanks to:

- The saints who have preceded me to heaven, from whose writing and teaching I have learned so much about worship, including Dr. Judson Cornwall, Dr. Robert Webber, A.W. Tozer, and, last but not least, the Apostle John.

- My good friend, Jerry Waggoner, for the great questions in the "Going Deeper" sections.

- Jennifer Brody, Diane Lopez, and Fran Moore, for editing and proofreading at various stages along the way.

- My wonderful wife and family for allowing me the time and encouraging me to write.

Contents

Prologue

My dad was an amazing mechanic. Even after he moved from the blue-collar field into a white-collar position, he still greatly enjoyed working on automobiles. Way back when I was still living with my parents, my dad was nearly always tinkering with someone's car in our garage. From everything I saw, as well as all that his family and close friends have said, I'm pretty sure he could have dismantled and reassembled an engine with his eyes closed. It was truly a gift.

Unfortunately, I inherited none of that gene. Zero. Zippo. Nada. I couldn't do auto repair if my life depended on it. I won't even tell you my horror stories of working on cars. Let's just say, they're not pretty. So when I need work done on a car, it goes to someone who knows what they're doing.

I remember years ago, our car was pulling strongly to one side. That pulling had gone on for awhile when I finally decided to take it to a mechanic. He patiently explained that the car was out of alignment. He showed me how the front tires were both worn on one side because of the tug to that side. Somehow, something had become misadjusted. He wondered if, perhaps, I had hit a pothole or something. The tire-wear would get worse, he assured me, unless the problem was fixed. I nodded and smiled, but inside I was genuinely excited, because it was one of the few mechanical things I had ever really understood.

When a car is out of alignment, it pulls to one side. The more the alignment is off, the more it pulls. It is difficult to make the car go in the right direction when the alignment is off.

Here's why I'm telling you this: I think the alignment is off in the Church, specifically in the area of worship. We're veering off course, and most of us don't even realize it. We're pulling to the side—leaders and followers alike—and we don't recognize it. Whether we know it or not, we need an alignment.

In this short book, I'll offer some explanations about how the alignment is off and also some ideas about what we can do to correct it. My hope and prayer is that recognizing the misalignment will cause us to make the necessary adjustments to correct it.

SECTION 1

WHAT IS WORSHIP IN HEAVEN LIKE?

Worship in Heaven: A Visit to the Source

The following is a fanciful story based on glimpses of worship in Heaven from John's Revelation. Afterward, we'll talk about what we saw in the story and what it means for us today.

The door bell rang. *Odd,* I thought. *Who would be at the door at this time of day?* My mind raced through the various possibilities, as I hurried to answer. *A delivery?* I wasn't expecting anything. *Mormons or Jehovah's Witnesses? More likely,* I thought. *Perhaps a neighbor needing something. Or maybe a salesperson with a new what's-it. Oh, I hope not.*

I opened the door only to realize that none of my imagined scenarios were correct. Instead, I found two middle-aged women standing before me. Both appeared to be of Middle Eastern descent, with black hair, dark eyes, and skin that was a few shades darker than mine. They seemed a bit nervous as they glanced about. Before I could ask what they wanted, though, the one to my right spoke.

"Hello. My name is Martha, and this is my sister." Her words were clear and distinct, but she had an obvious Middle Eastern accent. "I know this seems strange, but we need to tell you a story." She paused, again looking around nervously.

"A...*story?*" I repeated her words, doing my best to make the ridiculousness of my question sound obvious.

"Yes," she responded. "You see, our friend John..."

Just as she got going, her sister interrupted her. "John, our dear friend John..." This one spoke more rapidly than the other and with clear determination, "was living alone, and one day an angel appeared to him." She stopped and looked deep into my eyes, perhaps wondering if I was about to slam the door on them.

Martha gave her sister a scolding look that a sibling understands and then started in again, "John had an amazing vision, and..." She hesitated just a bit, then went on, "and our Lord has directed us here to share a part of that vision with you." She stopped again for just a second and then continued, "Apparently there's something in it that you really need to hear." Another hesitation, this time a bit longer, before she asked. "May we come in?"

I looked at Martha, then to her sister and back again. I really wasn't certain how to respond. Two strange—foreign, no less—women were asking to enter my home, to tell me about a heavenly message. This was light years from what I had expected when I answered the door. These two were either truly on a mission from God, or they were totally insane. I wavered for just a moment, as I pondered whether either of these possibilities might actually be true, or, if, perhaps, there was a third option that I was missing. Finally, I gave in and motioned for them to enter. I'll be honest, though, I questioned whether I would later regret my decision.

Through our front door is the living room. As the two women entered, they looked around the room as though they had never seen anything like it. You must understand that I don't live in an elaborate house. By American standards, our living room is smallish and decorated plainly. So their surprised reaction seemed pretty strange to me. *Who are these women, and where did they come from?* I wondered.

I directed Martha and her sister toward the couch, where they sat down. Before they sat, though, they fawned over the sofa. My wife and I had bought that couch before we were married more than thirty years ago. It's been reupholstered, but it really is nothing special. *It's just an ordinary couch*, I thought, as I took a seat on a chair opposite them.

There was a moment of nervous uncertainty, but then Martha spoke. "We don't really have time to tell you the *entire* story, but we'll recap just a little and then tell you the parts *you* really need to hear."

I have to admit, as I sat there, I wondered what was so all-fire important about me hearing certain parts of a story from their friend John. This was a little over the edge, even for an adventuresome guy like me. I was getting a bit antsy, but I tried my best to be patient.

"In the first part of the vision, the Lord spoke warnings and affirmations to the Church. He gave some important rebukes and a few encouragements. Things like, 'Don't be half-hearted' and 'Don't think you're something really special.'" She paused, then went on. "But then John saw Heaven."

"Actually, it was more like he was *taken* to Heaven," her sister interrupted. "John said he could see and feel and taste and know everything that was going on there in Heaven. It was definitely more than just seeing it. He was there." She smiled at Martha, and Martha smiled back.

"Mary is right about that," responded Martha, but the slight edge to her voice made me a bit concerned about whether this back and forth interruption would be happening the whole time they were there, and, if it did, would they start arguing?

Then it dawned on me. *Did she say, "Mary"? Is this Mary and Martha? Like, as in, Lazarus' sisters? But how could it be? Mary and Martha were friends of Jesus dur-*

ing His visible earthly ministry. They couldn't still be alive, could they?

As these thoughts whirled through my head, Martha continued. "John saw—maybe was transported to...we just don't know—Heaven. Somehow, he got glimpses of worship in Heaven." She looked directly at me. "You teach people about worshiping God, don't you?"

How does she know that, and how much more does she know about me? I wondered. "Uh, yes. That's correct. I teach in churches, and worship is my primary topic. But how did you..." I never got a chance to finish the question.

"Then you especially, of all people, need to understand what John saw," cut in Mary. "The scenes and descriptions may well change people's understanding of worship...maybe even yours." Mary caught sight of Martha out of the corner of her eye. "Uh oh," she said as she glanced from Martha and then back to me again. "I promised I would try to let Martha do most of the talking. So far I'm not doing very well, am I?" A nervous giggle escaped from her lips. She smiled at me, then at Martha, and then looked down at her lap, doing her best not to look embarrassed.

Her sister smiled. Martha seemed more proper than Mary, more rigid in her speaking. Mary, it appeared, liked to dive in head first, without much forethought. Martha apparently preferred everything to be neat and orderly. Her words were measured and careful; Mary's were spontaneous and impulsive.

Martha started in again. "John's description of the

scene in Heaven actually seems pretty outrageous. He kept grasping for words, trying to come up with an accurate description of what he saw." She paused and then continued thoughtfully, "The more he talked, though, the more he seemed to struggle."

Mary interrupted again. "I thought exactly the same thing. It was like he couldn't find the right words in our language to convey what he had seen. I got the impression that everything he said fell short in its description. Earthly language failed to communicate the heavenly scenes he had beheld. Words were just not adequate, and John was frustrated."

"Yes," responded Martha, "he certainly was." She stopped, looked up toward the ceiling for a moment, and then began again. "You have met people who have had what you call a "stroke," right?"

I nodded.

"Do you know how they sometimes struggle when they talk? They know the right word in their minds, but they're unable to verbalize it?"

I had, in fact, just a few days earlier, encountered that very scenario with a dear friend. I nodded again. "Yes," I responded.

"Well, that's how John seemed to be acting. He knew what he had seen—he remembered every moment vividly. Every detail was etched into his memory. It seemed as though God had supernaturally imprinted it into John's mind. But trying to communicate those scenes—trying to get others to envision what he had seen—well, that was a different matter entirely."

"Exactly," added Mary.

"To be honest," continued Martha, "I'm afraid Mary and I might have the same problem. We'll do our best, but we didn't actually see what John saw. We just have his words to go by—words that he thought were inadequate—so bear with us."

I smiled. I suddenly realized I was much more relaxed now. Maybe this wouldn't be so bad after all. "That's fine," I said. "You just talk, and if I have any questions or don't understand something, I'll ask. Okay?" *This is getting interesting*, I thought.

"Perfect," responded Martha. She started the story from the beginning, doing her best to choose each word carefully. But as she began to speak, something strange happened. Her words seemed to fade out; her mouth was moving but the sound got quieter and quieter. Then, suddenly, we heard an ear-splitting trumpet blast. Maybe it was a ram's horn. It could have been a trombone for all I know. Whatever the actual instrument, I do know it was really, *really* loud. And it wasn't just a polite, short little horn blast. It seemed to go on and on. I hoped it wouldn't wake up my next-door neighbor, who works nights.

While this deafening noise was blaring, no joke, the side of my house started to fall away. The wall just began to lean outward. It wasn't just the wall, though. The piano and the bookcase that were against the wall were leaning away from me, too. I didn't know if the horn blast was causing it, but I was worried that the roof was about to collapse on top of us. And I was really worried about my daughter's brand-new piano. However, as more and more of what was on the other side of the wall came into view, I realized I didn't need to be concerned about the roof or the piano. You see, outside—beyond the wall—didn't look like what was usually outside my house. Not at all. I knew what should be there—driveway, trees, yard, etc.—and this wasn't it. Not even close.

I stole a quick glance over at Martha and Mary. The looks on their faces told me they were clearly as astonished as I was. Their mouths hung open, and their eyes were as big as saucers. This disappearing wall trick was apparently not in their original plan.

When my wall was completely gone, we saw another wall, a huge wall of hand-polished wood—maybe something like mahogany or walnut—with ornate carvings on it. This wall was at least twenty feet tall, and right in the middle of it was an elaborately carved door...a door that was gradually opening.

I looked over again at the two women. They were no longer seated. Instead, they were slowly walking toward the carved door. Well, I certainly didn't want to miss out, so I followed them, albeit, a bit hesitantly at first. I wasn't sure what was going on, but I didn't want to be left out of an unfolding adventure.

As we moved forward, though, I noticed we weren't walking on our living room carpet or even our driveway, which should have been right outside the missing wall. Instead, we walked on brightly polished marble that spread out in all directions. I'm no expert on home furnishings, but this sure looked to me like the real thing. It wasn't vinyl or even ceramic tiles pretending to be marble. *But how did I get a marble floor?* I wondered. Strange, the things that run through one's mind at inopportune times.

As we walked through the door, I unexpectedly found myself thinking about being at Disney World years before. Our family was there for a few days, but after just the first few hours, the special effects caused me to question what was real and what wasn't real almost every moment we were there. I found myself wondering the same thing now. *Was this real? Was I just dreaming?*

As we hurried through the doorway, I realized that the room was huge. I couldn't even see the far wall. It could have been miles away, for all I knew. Nor could I see the ceiling. If this was a room, it was far more enormous than any room—or even stadium—I had ever been in.

Out of the corner of my eye, I noticed Martha staring off to the right. I turned my gaze to the direction she was looking, and there I saw a huge throne. But the word "throne" may not do it justice. This was much more elaborate than any throne I'd ever seen in any movie. Forget the thrones of King Arthur or even the Elf King. Those were silly little anemic thrones by comparison. Think of the grandest throne you can, and then multiply to make it 10,000 times more grand and you might be getting close. This throne was made of solid gold, and the ornamental scroll-work was embedded with the largest and finest of jewels imaginable. When I was a boy, I once saw the Hope

Diamond, the largest blue diamond in the world. These beauties made that marvelous gem seem paltry. This was definitely unlike any human throne could ever be.

Still the throne was nothing compared to the One who sat on it. He looked young and old at the same time. He seemed innocent, but had an air of wisdom and understanding. He appeared regal and majestic, but also plain and humble. To this day, I have no idea how those attributes could all have been wrapped into one being, but they were. And so much more that words could never describe. I began to understand why John had such trouble verbalizing his vision.

Did I mention that the One on the throne glowed? I don't mean like when we talk about a bride or an expectant mother—"She fairly glowed." No, He actually *glowed*. There was a very real luminous radiance. Light emitted from Him. The glow was a rainbow of light that seemed to change and vary with each passing second, yet it wasn't gaudy or carnival-ish. Not in the least. In fact, it looked regal, majestic.

I've heard people who have seen angels say that they glow. Maybe they do, but this was no angel. Lightning flashed from Him. It sparked out in all directions. The low rumbling of the peals of thunder made any surround-sound theater I've ever encountered seem lifeless and hollow. The majesty and grandeur, the splendor and magnificence, were unmistakable. This was God Almighty seated on His throne.

I just stared, unable to speak. Never mind speak, I realized I hadn't even drawn a breath since I walked through the door. Honestly, I wondered if I would ever breathe again. Maybe I would never *need* to breathe again.

Then the song, "I Can Only Imagine," started echoing in my head. Again, the things that run through my mind can be downright bizarre at times. *Weird*, I thought. *I no longer need to imagine. I'm actually here.* I immediately realized, though, that I was there more as an observer than as a participant. *I guess I'll still need to imagine for a while longer.*

As my gaze broadened, I saw twenty-four other thrones around the big one, all facing in toward the middle. These thrones were still more elaborate than any I've seen before, but they were insignificant compared to the main one. On each of these thrones sat an older-looking human being with a simple gold crown, and each was wearing a dazzlingly white robe. I'm pretty sure that in another setting the brilliance of the white would have been startling. Here, near to the brightness of God, they seemed lackluster, even bordering on being dull.

Then I noticed that between me and the thrones was a gleaming lake. This was no ordinary lake, though. (As if, at this point, that should surprise me.) The small ripples on the surface were stuck in place; they didn't move. It wasn't cold enough to be frozen over, so it looked as though the lake was made of glass. Actually, the way it shimmered, maybe crystal would be a better description. Although it appeared to be solid, I still recognized it as a lake. I wondered if Peter and John—or even my dad—ever got to go fishing there. Then I realized that such a thing might not really be appropriate.

I'm not sure if my eyes were still adjusting to the light or what, but different parts of the scene kept popping out to me. The sight I beheld next, though, was really strange. Four creatures surrounded the great throne. They were closer than the twenty-four thrones, which made me wonder why I hadn't noticed them earlier, but they were, uh, different. *Really* different. Over the top different.

One of them looked sort of like a lion. The one next to him looked kind of like an ox. The next one appeared almost human. The last one resembled an eagle. But—and here's where it got weird—they all had eyes. Not that eyes in general are weird, but they didn't have eyes like you and I have eyes. I'm talking about many eyes. Lots of eyes. Lots and lots of eyes. Covered with eyes, front and back. Eyes everywhere. I told you it was strange.

That's not even the whole story. You see, each of those four creatures had six wings. I saw a movie once with this creepy flying creature that had four wings. That was strange enough, but these guys had six wings each. Bizarre, huh? Yet, it gets even more unusual. Each of their six wings was covered with eyes. Underneath. On top. All around. Covered. Wings with hundreds of eyes. Steven Spielberg, or even the entire Pixar team, couldn't have dreamed this one up.

I know my mom had eyes in the back of her head, but this was *way* beyond that. I wondered how they knew what they were looking at. What type of brain did they have to be able to control all those eyes? Perhaps, here in Heaven, all those eyes were necessary to take in the entire scene. It certainly is possible.

Then, just when I thought the scene could not stray any farther into abnormal territory, it did. Those four creatures talked. Each of them spoke, and they spoke words that I understood. I was okay with the human-looking guy talking. That was not terribly unsettling. But the lion, the ox, and the eagle, too? I started wondering if at any minute Tumnus the Fawn would come walking through. This had to be a dream. At least I thought so, until I heard what they were saying. "Holy, holy, holy is the Lord God, the Almighty—the One who always was, who is, and who is still to come."[1] Their deep resonant voices shook the floor. And they didn't just say this once. Over and over again, they kept chanting the same thing. They were certainly not in a hurry as they said it, but the words echoed again and again. "Holy, holy, holy is the Lord God, the Almighty—the One who always was, who is, and who is still to come." Years later, I can still hear the exact words thundering through the recesses of my mind.

I know some people have told me that when they repeat something a few times—say, the chorus to a song during a worship service—they'll sometimes start to zone out. Saying the same thing over and over seems to lose something for them. Someone once said that oft-repeated words can become empty words. In general, I would have a tendency to agree with that statement, but the repetition in this setting certainly didn't seem to make any difference for these odd creatures. It almost seemed as though the more they repeated the words, the more they believed them. The words became a part of them. This was truth, and their growing recognition of that truth was communicated in the way they said it. "Holy, holy, holy is the Lord God, the Almighty—the One who always was, who is, and who is still to come." The intensity grew each time. Those words seemed to have more and more life with each subsequent repetition.

Then I noticed another twist. As the four strange-looking creatures worshiped, so did the twenty-four elders. They fell facedown, prostrate, and laid their gold crowns before God's throne. As they did this, they cried out, "You are worthy, O Lord our God, to receive glory and honor and power." There was a very slight pause, and then they continued, "For you created all things, and they exist because you created what you pleased."[2]

Their part in this drama seemed oddly reminiscent of the four creatures. Don't misunderstand. They did and said something totally different. It was certainly no mirror image. There was no mimicking going on. But, just like the four creatures, they did it over and over and over. "You are worthy, O Lord our God, to receive glory and honor and power. For you created all things, and they exist because you created what you pleased." Their words intermingled with those of the four creatures and echoed through Heaven's chambers. With each repetition, the intensity seemed to increase. These words were clearly not just some rehearsed script they quoted in an effort to appease

God. It was obvious that these guys meant—and meant passionately—every word they said.

As I listened to their words again and again, I was struck by both the simplicity and the depth. They declared that God was worthy, and they hailed Him as the Creator. That was pretty much the summation of what they said. Nevertheless, the repetition caused me to ponder the words. Indeed, as the One Who made everything, He is the only One laudable enough to receive glory and honor and power. No wonder they bowed before Him in worship and laid their crowns at His feet. As I listened, I recognized that I, too, was part of the creation that He was pleased to make. As that truth took hold inside me, I found myself joining in the refrain, "You are worthy, O Lord our God, to receive glory and honor and power. For You created all things, and they exist because You created what You pleased." I, too, bowed in worship before my Creator.

Although Mary, Martha, and I were all caught up in worshiping the Lord, we also knew that we were primarily there as observers in order to learn. As I glanced toward the two women, seated just a few feet from where I was, they were whispering. They motioned for me to join them.

"This is at least part of what I was talking about earlier," whispered Mary. "The inhabitants of Heaven don't talk about—or even think about—themselves. Their worship doesn't include any selfish thoughts or actions; it's all pointed toward the Lord. I have to think that such a notion is as different in your culture as it is in ours. As human beings, we are so self-centered. Unlike us, though, these folks here are totally focused on God."

I had to agree. This was definitely different than any of my experiences on Earth.

Then Martha added, "When our Lord taught His disciples to pray, He told them to pray, 'Your will be done on earth as it is in heaven.' At least a part of what He meant by that was that what we do and think and say on Earth should be aligning more and more with the pattern of Heaven. 'On earth as in heaven.' Our lives and actions should mirror the things happening in Heaven. In other words, Heaven should be our model, our example. And, if you think about it, this has to include our worship." She paused for a thoughtful moment and then continued, "Perhaps *especially* our worship."

"Exactly," chimed in Mary. "We need to be vigilant about shoving aside the selfish ideas and thoughts that we are so inclined toward, and, instead, center our focus squarely on only the Lord Himself. Anything less misses the pattern we see here in Heaven."

I nodded again in agreement. I realized that, just as Mary had predicted earlier, this encounter was certainly changing my thinking. Would I ever be able to look at any words of worship—any songs or liturgies—from the same perspective as I had before? I recognized how selfish and self-centered were the words that I had sung and spoken in the past. I knew that just what I had witnessed here in Heaven so far was greatly altering my frame of reference. Little did I realize then, that this was only the beginning of what ultimately would be a seismic shift inside of me.

We looked back toward the throne, and the scene shifted. Don't ask me how a scene just changes in real life. I know how it happens in movies and, occasionally, in live theater, but this was different. This wasn't a movie or a theatrical production, so how it happened, I don't know. It just...changed.

A scroll appeared in God's hand. Out of nowhere, it just suddenly appeared. I couldn't tell anything about the contents of the scroll, but I could plainly see that it was sealed with royal-looking seals. Then, just as quickly as the scroll had appeared, an enormous angel also appeared. He looked about, as though searching for something, but apparently he couldn't find it. So, without warning, he yelled loudly, "Is there anyone who can open the scroll, who can break its seals?"[3] His booming voice echoed off the walls and shook me to the core.

Then silence. Long, still silence. No response. Not the slightest sound.

Surely, I thought, *there must be someone among this group who could open a scroll. Anyone?*

Nothing. Just more overwhelming noiselessness.

I don't know how or why, but all of sudden I was keenly aware—supernaturally aware?—that opening the scroll was a big deal. A *really* big deal. I don't know if it was just the emotion of the moment or the combination of everything that I had seen so far, but I started crying. If no one could open the scroll, what did it mean? I wasn't completely certain, but I knew it wasn't good. So I wept. As I looked over at Mary and Martha, I saw that they, too, were crying.

Remembering back now, I wish I had a video of that scene. The three of us lying on the floor, weeping. It must have been an odd sight. Although I'm not entirely certain, after everything else we had experienced there, that this truly would have fallen into the "strange" category. But I digress.

Suddenly, as I lay there on the marble floor, I was vaguely aware of someone standing near us. Out of the corner of my eye I recognized that it was one of the elders from one of the thrones. He had taken leave of his throne and strode over to us. I immediately pondered that perhaps we *were* making more of scene than necessary, but when I looked up at him, he said, "Do not weep! See, the Lion of the tribe of Judah, the Root of David, has triumphed. He is able to open the scroll."[4]

As his words sank in, I knew immediately that I should look back toward the throne. Sure enough, there on the main throne was a Lamb. This was no ordinary lamb, though. (After all I had seen there, I was beginning to wonder if I could ever call anything "ordinary" again.) This Lamb had seven horns and seven eyes. That by itself was peculiar enough, but as I looked at the Lamb, somehow I knew that it had been slaughtered; its lifeblood had been spilled. Yet there it was, alive and standing tall.

I don't know about your dreams, but in mine, sometimes things morph into something else, sort of like the Transformers do. I recall one dream in which I was driving our old family van, and it suddenly changed into a brand new Mazda Miata. Nice! Inexplicable things like that happen in dreams. They don't tend to happen in real life. Well, not usually.

As I watched, the Lamb—the Lamb I distinctly remember seeing *on* the throne—now walked *over* to the throne and took the scroll from the One who sat on the throne. (I know it doesn't seem to make sense, but I'm just describing what I saw.) When He took the scroll, the four creatures and all the elders fell down before the Lamb. Not only did they fall down, but somehow all twenty-eight of them now each had a harp and a gold bowl full of incense. I don't know for sure if they were actually *playing* the harps. I didn't notice their fingers strumming or plucking. I do know that the most glorious music I've ever heard was emanating from the harps. The sweet, rich fragrance of the incense wafted through the room, somehow mixing and intertwining with the music. The sound and the aroma almost became one.

I'm sure that what I'm writing here falls far short of what I actually saw there. I understand even more now what Martha meant when she said that John had struggled to describe what he had seen. These simple words are nowhere close to an apt description. There really aren't adequate words to paint the full picture. I'm pretty sure you would have needed to be there to fully comprehend it.

Then, as the music and incense rose toward the throne, the instrumental harp music somehow begged for vocal accompaniment. So the elders and creatures sang a simple yet profound new song to the Lamb:

> Worthy are you to take the scroll
> and to open its seals,
> for you were slain,
> and by your blood you ransomed people for God
> from every tribe and language
> and people and nation,
> and you have made them
> a kingdom and priests to our God,
> and they shall reign on the earth.[5]

I'm sure that the words alone, without the music and incense, lose something. It was far more majestic than words on a piece of paper can convey. The intermingling of the amazing visuals, the powerful sounds, and the wonderful smells created an overwhelmingly inspiring experience.

As I watched and listened, I couldn't help thinking that this did not seem scripted or rehearsed. It was spontaneous, a right-on-the-spot, brand-new song, coming directly from their hearts. Yet, they all sang it together, this new song, loaded with thanksgiving and praise for the Lamb, the One Who had been slain.

As I watched the scene unfold, I, too, joined in with their worship, honoring the Lamb Who had ransomed *me*. The experience was both glorious and overwhelming. However, I found out quickly, this was just the beginning.

Out of nowhere, appeared thousands upon thousands of angels. These weren't the cute little cherub angels you see in cartoons or on Christmas cards. No, there was not a single runt in the whole bunch. These were the angels you want protecting you. Big. Strong. Powerful. There were more of them than I could possibly count. As far as the eye could see, angels, angels, and more angels. There must have been millions of them. Together they lifted their voices and cried out, "Worthy is the Lamb who was slaughtered—to receive power and riches and wisdom and strength and honor and glory and blessing."[6] I thought the one angel shouting by himself earlier was loud. This time the ground shook from the force of so many strong voices in unison extolling the Lamb.

Then I heard every creature, not just the ones I could see, but *every* creature *everywhere*—all the angels and elders and the four creatures, along with all the people and animals of Earth, and even the sea creatures—all of them together, as one, declared, "Blessing and honor and glory and power be to Him who sits on the throne, and to the Lamb, forever and ever!"[7]

As the last word echoed thunderously through Heaven, the four creatures called out in a loud voice, "Amen!" Then the twenty-four elders bowed down in worship of the Lamb. The smooth marble floor felt cool against my forehead as I, too, paid homage to the risen Lamb.

As the reverberations of that final "Amen" dwindled, in contrast to the noise we had just heard, the great hall was now relatively silent. Silent, that is, except for the continuous whispers of adoration directed toward the

Lamb. "All glory to You!" "Praise be to the Lamb forever!" "Glory, glory...all glory belongs only to You, Jesus!" Everywhere creatures uttered their own words of worship to the Lamb.

My mind immediately flashed back to a beautifully ornate Hindu temple in Calcutta, India. Full frame into my mind raced the image of a young goat that had just been slaughtered. Blood from the sliced neck poured out onto the temple floor. A young man, perhaps in his mid-twenties, stood in the middle of the growing pool of blood. I watched as his face contorted into signs of agony and perhaps hopelessness; his shoulders heaved as he sobbed uncontrollably. Slowly, deliberately, looking as though he was in tremendous pain, he reached forward, still shaking from head to toe, and took hold of the blood-covered horns of the altar. He gripped them so tightly I was sure they would break off. He knew he needed something and he hoped—oh, how he hoped—that this act of penance would absolve him from his wretched sins and failures. As the scene unfolded, an elderly priest in ceremonial garb approached the young man—still clinging tightly to the horns of the altar—chanting a purification incantation over him. When the priest finished his chant, there was a brief moment of silence. Then he stretched out his hand and demanded an offering from the young man.

What a mind-boggling juxtaposition. On the one hand was a desperate young man trying to find peace through the blood of an earthly animal and the monetary compensation of an earthly priest. On the other hand, this heavenly scene before me depicted the result of the *true* sacrifice of the *true* Lamb. No begging and pleading. No exchange of a worldly offering (bribe?!). Just real forgiveness, because of the once-and-for-all sacrifice of the Lamb of God. Then, as a result, wholehearted, unabashed worship.

Truly the Lamb of God is worthy! I knelt there on the floor, listening to the quiet words uttered from thankful hearts, and I added my own voice to theirs in worship. "Thank You, Jesus, for Your sacrifice...for willingly laying down Your life...How good You are!"

I'm not sure how long we worshiped there together, but when I looked up again, the scene had changed once more. This time, along with the four creatures, the elders, and the angels, there were people, just regular everyday folks like you and me. Some were short, and some were tall; some were male, and some were female, but there were no extra eyes and no wings. Two legs, two arms, one head. Plain human beings. Lots of them. Many, many people. A veritable sea of humanity. The farther away I looked, the more people I saw. I felt like my eyes were straining to try to see the end of crowd, but I couldn't. They went on and on. Far more people than I have ever seen in one place before. Easily millions upon millions of people had gathered at the throne.

Please don't think of the vast hordes in the Star Wars Clone Wars where each soldier looked the same as the others, like cookie-cutter cutouts. No, this was a mixture of every ethnic group on Earth. I saw various Chinese,

Japanese, and many other Asian groups. Blacks from Africa, Australia, America, and other parts of the world. Polynesian, Hispanic, Caucasian, Middle Eastern, Native Americans...on and on, far too many to name. Somehow I knew that they not only looked different, but that they also spoke different languages. Every tribe from every nation had at least someone represented. At least one person was there from every people group throughout the earth. These were the saints of God, whom He Himself had rescued and redeemed for His glory. I was reminded of Psalm 86:9, "All the nations you have made shall come and worship before you, O Lord...."

Although every person looked unique—just the way God had created them—they were all dressed identically. Each one wore a white robe. I've seen white robes in church Easter productions. Jesus wears a white robe after the resurrection. Angels wear white robes showing their holiness or purity. However, these white robes were *far* whiter than any I've ever encountered on Earth. Brilliantly white, way beyond anything chlorine bleach could do. Each person in that vast sea of people—some dark-skinned, some light-skinned, some in between—was wearing a pure white garment. Also, they were all holding palm branches, just like the welcoming committee had held when Jesus rode into Jerusalem on a donkey. The multicolored faces, the amazingly white robes, the bright green palm branches—it was an exquisitely festive sight.

Just then, I felt something touch my arm. It was Martha. She leaned toward me and whispered, "Do you see it? Every one of these millions and millions of people is transfixed."

I looked back at the scene, and she was right. There was no doubt in my mind. Their joy-filled singular focus was unmistakable.

Then Mary leaned in from the other side. "They aren't looking around. They aren't talking with each other. There is not one person glancing at something off to the side or staring off into space. No one is giving a single thought to what time this whole 'ordeal' might be finished." She smiled.

"That's right," echoed Martha. "No one is complaining about having to stand for so long. Not a single one of these things even slightly matters to them."

It was quite the contrast to congregational worship I've seen. No one was yawning due to boredom or even tiredness. No one checked their watch. In the life-giving presence of God Almighty, there was no room for being bored or tired. Such things would have been entirely foreign in this environment. Then I added my own thoughts, "It also looks to me that, even though they're all dressed identically, none of them even realizes it. That's not even a blip on their radar."

Martha looked puzzled. "Blip?" she asked. "Radar?"

"Oh, sorry." I paused, thinking through other options for words, then continued, "No one is concerned that their outfit—what they're wearing—is just like someone else's."

Martha smiled knowingly, and Mary chimed in, "Of

course not. I don't think any of them even notices whether or not the others are even here."

She was correct again. There was a definite lack of self-awareness. As if they were one person, all eyes were fixed on the One on the throne. Their gazes were focused on God, the Savior.

I also found it fascinating to think that most of the things the average Christian talks about looking forward to in Heaven were not even apparent. Ask most believers about what they expect in Heaven, and you'll hear about being reunited with loved ones. Some will talk of having a new body and no more pain. Others will mention an end to sorrow and tears. Some look forward to a place where nothing breaks down or wears out—no repairs or replacements. Although all of those things are true, this crowd wasn't thinking about any of those. No, their one and only focus was the spotless Lamb of God, Who had redeemed them.

Then, as if on cue, they all shouted out loudly together, "Salvation comes from our God who sits on the throne and from the Lamb!"[8] Wow! It was a tremendous statement for them to utter together, and it was another thunderously powerful sound that seemed to echo on and on and on. The relentless intensity made me wonder if I would survive this day.

As I listened to the words, I was reminded of Psalm 3:8, "Salvation comes from the Lord,"[9] and Acts 4:12, "no other name under heaven given among men by which we must be saved."[10] This throng of people was right. Truly salvation comes only from God and the Lamb!

Just as the final echo of their words faded, the great horde of angels—they had been standing by, as the sea of people worshiped—were suddenly caught up in the moment. They all fell on their faces before the throne, and they, too, now worshiped. The angels cried out, "Amen! Blessing and glory and wisdom and thanksgiving and honor and power and might be to our God forever and ever! Amen."[11]

Again, I could barely breathe. Such purity. Such wholehearted adoration. No prompting was necessary. No script was needed. They declared their worship spontaneously from the depths of their beings. I was awed and humbled, and their worship caused me, again, to bow in worship before the throne of God.

Honestly, I'm not entirely certain how long I lay there prostrate before my Savior. It could have been minutes, maybe hours, perhaps even days. It made no difference. Time seemed irrelevant, as though it no longer existed. Gradually, though, I became aware of the steady ticking of a clock. *Strange,* I thought. The sound was so out of place. At the same moment, though, I also realized that I was no longer on a palatial marble floor. Instead, I was lying on carpet, carpet that looked very familiar. I looked up. and I was back in my own living room...alone.

Worship in Heaven: What's Normal?

I trust that you recognize the previous story as merely a creative retelling of a few small segments of the book of Revelation. Martha and Mary did not actually come to my door. Often in my teaching I have alluded to the glimpses of worship we see in Revelation. This is simply an imaginary visit to some of those brief glimpses. It's my attempt to help us visualize today what John saw back then.

Some time ago, I felt a need to write such a fictional rendition. In order to prepare for the writing, I read and reread sections of Revelation in various translations of the

Bible. As I read the scenes from more than a dozen different versions, I tried to picture them in my mind, doing my best to "see" what John saw. In my imagining, I was repeatedly struck by the depiction of the heavenly worship. In so many ways, it is radically different from what we describe as worship here on Earth.

Allow me a moment to try to illustrate what I'm talking about.

Our daughter had heart surgery last year. We didn't even know there was a problem until she passed out. We were sitting in a restaurant in a very remote area in another country. One second Amy was talking to her mom, and the next second she slumped over in her chair, out cold. I picked her up and carried her outside, praying all the way. After a couple of hours she was pretty much back to normal, but she sure gave us a scare. There wasn't a hospital anywhere even close to us.

Amy had passed out a couple of other times years ago. Doctors could never find a problem, so we just let it go. This was a biggie, though, and it caused us great concern. So lots of tests ensued, including Amy wearing a heart monitor for a month. She loved that one...or not.

The physicians did, however, determine that she has an arrhythmia. Her heart just starts to race. No apparent reason. It just takes off. The heart monitor revealed at least one episode during that month where Amy's heart rate was nearly 200 beats per minute. She wasn't doing anything to cause it. No running or heavy lifting. Something just clicks and the heart goes wild.

As we discussed it, Amy told us that she has this happen often. In fact, it had been happening as far back as she could remember.

"So, why did you never tell us?" we asked her.

"Why would I?" she responded. "I just thought it was normal."

That's when the light went on in my mind. She had never known anything different. She had no idea that everyone else didn't experience the same thing. She had no reason to realize that these racing-heart episodes were not something that everybody encountered. For Amy, it was normal.

In much the same way, I think all of us live in a subpar manner most of the time. Sin has marred our existence here on Earth. Nowhere is this more evident than in the arena of worship. What we call worship falls so far short of the heavenly pattern that I have to wonder whether we even understand a small inkling of true worship. But for us, what we have experienced is normal. Just like Amy's racing heart, it's all we've ever known. Maybe, just maybe, there's something more, something different, something closer to the worship in Heaven.

Since I was challenged by what I observed in those glimpses of worship from John's Revelation, I wrote this simply to cause us to ponder honestly the issue of worship. I certainly am not trying to add to, or take anything away from, the overall message of Revelation.[12] In fact, with the obvious exception of Mary, Martha, and me, most of the rest can be found either directly in the text or at least inferred by the text.

So, if we really understand what we've just read, if we truly recognize how extremely different worship is in Heaven than it is here on Earth, then there is a looming question that needs to be addressed: Why is there such a vast difference between worship on Earth and worship in Heaven? In other words, what are the reasons for the stark contrast between worship here and worship there?

Further, I have become convinced that honestly addressing this question can cause our worship here and now to become richer and more complete. Recognizing the reasons for the discrepancy and taking actions to counteract those reasons will, in many respects, reform our worship. And make no mistake, if we are indeed so very far from the true pattern, then our worship needs reforming.

So let's take a look at some of the reasons, as well as some practical ideas to change us, as individuals and also on the congregational level.

GOING DEEPER

- Have you ever had an experience, like the one Tom describes about his daughter, in which you realized that something you thought was "normal" was really quite abnormal?
- Can you give an example of a time when studying Scripture made you change your view of what was "normal" in a way that changed your thinking?

Worship on Earth Is Practice for Worship in Heaven

I don't know about your reaction to reading the words in Revelation that depict the worship of Heaven, but when I read those sections, I can't help but notice the singular fixation. There appears to be no distractedness—not even anything *to* distract the attention. It is almost as though nothing beyond the worshipers exists, except God. They are solely focused on Him and Him alone.

When we—you and I—reach that grand and glorious day and we first enter Heaven, we will be so overwhelmed by the glory of God that nothing else will matter. All former anxiety, trepidation, apprehension and fear will be thrust aside. There will be no guilt tapping us on the shoulder, vying for our attention. All "what-ifs" and "if-onlys" will disappear. No thoughts drifting toward inappropriate or irrelevant ideas or memories. The totality of our awareness will be centered on the One on the throne. Nothing else will matter then.

Yet, the truth is that that day is still somewhere in the future. It's not here, not yet. It's not now. It will come, but for now that experience is still somewhere on the horizon. We can think and dream about it, but it is still off in the distance somewhere. Here and now we still struggle with guilt and worry and people and relationships and sin and...on and on.

Undeniably, there are qualitative differences between Heaven and Earth. In Heaven, we won't need to confess the truth of God's Word by calling things that are not as though they are, like we do here. In Heaven we will somehow "see" God; here and now we can only imagine Him. In Heaven, all distractions will have been taken away; on Earth we will always struggle with competing thoughts and distracting ideas. In Heaven there will be no sinful desires or impulses; here such things abound.

The differences between Heaven and Earth are myriad. The contrast is stark and obvious. So, if we're completely honest, worship here on Earth will never perfectly mirror the worship of Heaven. It can't. The two places are simply too far apart in nearly every respect. As a result, there will always be fundamental, intrinsic differences.

So does this mean we give up on trying to emulate the worship that we see depicted in Heaven? No! That would be like giving up on the sanctification process merely because we will never reach perfection here on Earth. By God's grace, we keep pressing forward in the strength of the Holy Spirit to see our lives more and more mirror the Christian life we see in Scripture. We should do the same with worship. Now that we've seen and recognized the goal, we push toward it. Of course, because of the qualitative differences between Heaven and Earth, we won't actually reach that goal here on Earth, but the goal keeps us moving forward. It helps propel us in the right direction.

Additionally, in some ways, our worship here and now helps prepare us for worship in Heaven. If worship has been an unwelcome intruder in this earthly life, then Heaven may immediately seem even more foreign to us than it would otherwise.

Over the years, my family and I have gone on some wonderful family vacations. Whitewater rafting in Colorado. Frolicking in the ocean off the coast of Maine. Sea World and Epcot Center in Florida, the Grand Canyon, the Statue of Liberty, and more, have been exciting destinations and made lots of fun memories.

When our family decides to take a vacation, we typically do hours of research to be sure to take advantage of every opportunity. Lots of forethought goes into exactly where we're going and what we will do once we're there. We study the attractions in the area, overnight accommodations, restaurants, and entertainment possibilities. We find out about nearby churches. In short, we try to make informed choices, so that our vacation is a positive experience for each of us. We plan and prepare as much as possible beforehand.

In light of this, I have to wonder how many Christians actually take the time to consider their ultimate destination. What will Heaven be like? What will our worship be like there? Is what we're doing here preparing us for that experience? And if not, why not?

I happened across a blogger's quote that seems pertinent here: "The Christian's life should be a dress rehearsal on earth for an eternity of worship in heaven."[13] Worship on Earth is practice for worship in Heaven. Our worship here and now, in some ways, prepares us for worship in eternity.

Just because our worship here on Earth will never reach the perfection of Heaven's worship, that is no reason to ignore or short-change worship here and now. It is, and should be, a vital part of our experience on Earth. We should see worship on Earth as preparation—a dress rehearsal—for Heaven. We should keep pressing toward the goal of God's will being done here on Earth as it is in Heaven.

GOING DEEPER

- Jesus teaches us to pray, "Thy will be done on earth as it is in heaven." How might this prayer pertain to Tom's assertion that we should be emulating heavenly worship?

• Why will having the goal of emulating heavenly worship help us, even though we will never actually attain it perfectly?

Worship in Heaven Is a Group Activity

I would challenge you to take another look at the scenes of worship in Heaven. Read through them again. One of the primary things that stands out to me is that they are corporate. By that, I mean that the group as a whole is doing the same thing at the same time. Of course, as we read through the book of Revelation, we see the overall scene unfolding. The exact same thing is not happening the entire time. However, when something does happen, it is not just one person doing it. There is always a group, a collection of folks, doing it together. The four living creatures. The twenty-four elders. The host of angels. The myriad of saints. There seems to be no individual aspect to Heaven.

In our society, the individual is prized. In the minds of most people, their needs and wants trump the needs and wants of others. As a culture, we are horrendously selfish. This is true even in the Church, despite the fact that we are told to "count others more significant than yourselves" (Philippians 2:3). No matter what Scripture says, we want what we want, and we'll do whatever we want, whenever we want.

In our fleshly nature, that's true of me...and you, too. Now don't sit there getting upset with me because I just said that about you. I'm merely giving voice to what everyone else already knows is true. If you don't believe me, put down this book and go ask your spouse or your parents or your kids or your best friends. Ask them if you have any selfish tendencies. I'll wait, because it won't take long to get an answer. If you *always* count others as more significant than yourself, then perhaps I'm not speaking to you. But since you don't, I guess I really am referring to you, after all.

So what does this have to do with worship? Everything.

Christian pollster George Barna said it like this, "A growing obstacle to genuine worship is the rampant individualism that characterizes so much of our society." You see, having lived with that individualistic mindset throughout the rest of the week, we have a tendency then to bring such thinking into the congregational worship setting. No matter that everyone else is standing, I don't feel like standing up right now. Or, in spite of the fact that the congregation is praying *together* at the moment, I need to check the messages on my phone or look at my watch to see how long this is taking. I may do some other activity that distracts me from what we're doing *together* as a church body. Of course, I'm sure *you* would never do any of these things....

I see it all the time as I travel. The person leading worship during the service may make a simple request like, "If you're able, would you lift your hands right now to the Lord as an act of surrender?" Then what happens? Perhaps two-thirds of the people, at best, will raise their hands. Usually, it's less than half. Perhaps the leader asks the congregation to kneel down, or something as basic as to sing along. The participation level is still relatively dismal.

Keep in mind that it's certainly not that all the rest of the people are incapable of raising their hands or singing. They just don't want to. Some say, "I'm too tired." Others would suggest, "I don't see the point." Some might be totally honest and admit, "I just don't feel like it." Or, one of my favorites, "I don't want to make a spectacle of myself." (Actually, if everyone else is doing it, and you're not, you're making more of a spectacle of yourself by *not* raising your hands.) It is an individualistic mindset that is completely and totally foreign to the worshipers in Heaven.

Of course, as we've already discussed, the worship of Heaven is intrinsically different from worship on Earth. Apparently, in Heaven, no one needs to be told what to do. It almost seems that worshiping in a commingled way is natural for the inhabitants of Heaven. They just do it—together—with no one offering instructions or guidance. It appears that worship there is innately done collectively, en masse. Unfortunately, that's not the case here on Earth.

There is, however, plenty of scriptural precedent for worshiping in a unified manner and even for leaders to offer specific leadership for worshipers to join in together. In Nehemiah 9:5, the Levites told the people who were gathered, "Stand up and bless the LORD your God..." The leaders were guiding them as to how to respond together. The writer of Psalm 134:2, tells the people to "Lift up your hands...bless the LORD!" That's not a command for one or two, or even a select few. It's clearly aimed at a group, those who would sing that song (psalm) together. Earlier in the book of Psalms we are told, "Oh come, let us worship and bow down; let us kneel before the LORD, our Maker!" (Psalm 95:6). Again, this is obviously meant to be a unified response from the people.

Please understand that I am certainly not asking you, necessarily, to like or be excited about what I'm saying here. However, I am suggesting that just as we allow Scripture to inform and guide our lives in general, we also must allow Scripture to inform and guide the way that we worship. If we don't, we're left to our own selfishness to decide what is appropriate and what is not.

From an honest biblical perspective, there is—and should be—a corporateness to our corporate worship. When we gather as a congregation, we should act like a congregation, not just a bunch of individuals all doing their own thing. We see it clearly in the worship in the heavenly realms. Our autonomous individual culture can, too often, cause us to miss the corporate aspect of worship. Instead of allowing that to happen—instead of giving in to our own selfish nature—we should push back by recognizing and attempting to mirror the unified worship we see in Heaven.

GOING DEEPER

- How significant/important is it that we worship as a group?
- Do you agree with Barna's assertion that "rampant individualism" is "a growing obstacle to genuine worship"? Why or why not?
- Are the heavenly worshipers thinking about, or mindful of, the group, or are they absorbed in the One Whom they are worshiping?

Worship in Heaven Is Diverse

I love trying to picture this scene in my mind: "After this I looked, and behold, a great multitude that no one could number, from every nation, from all tribes and peoples and languages, standing before the throne and before the Lamb, clothed in white robes, with palm branches in their hands, and crying out with a loud voice, 'Salvation belongs to our God who sits on the throne, and to the Lamb!'" (Revelation 7:9-10).

With even the slightest bit of imagination, that's

quite the scene. People of every ethnicity gathered as one. Every culture from around the globe represented. Each language—currently nearly 7,000 different ones have been identified worldwide. All skin colors, from the darkest black pigmentation to the palest white and everything in between. All together for a single purpose: to glorify God Almighty. What a picture!

As I have mentally envisioned this scene many times, I can't help but add some details that John doesn't mention. (Not that they weren't present, just that he doesn't mention them.) First, among those multitudes, there must also have been different sizes of people. Even though we will all have new heavenly bodies there, I don't get the impression that we will all suddenly have cookie-cutter bodies, each exactly the same size and shape. Even apart from the obvious gender differences, some people are just generally bigger than others. Weight issues aside, some folks are bigger-boned and are simply larger than others. I have difficulty imagining that our 5'1" daughter and our 6'8" family friend will suddenly be the same size in heaven. There clearly must be different sizes involved in this scene.

That idea leads into my other observation that John doesn't mention: different ages represented. Some people have suggested that, in heaven, we will all be roughly the same age. That's a nice theory, but I don't see any biblical support for this idea. Further, I find it unfathomable that my mother, who passed on to glory at age 81, will suddenly be the same age as the deceased two-year-old daughter of our dear friends.

The fact that John mentions neither of these concepts—size or age—does not mean they were not present. Consider this: from John's perspective, as a good Jewish boy telling this story, various ethnicities were a huge stretch. To John, this must have been similar to Peter's vision on the rooftop, when God sent him to the Gentiles (Acts 9). For someone who had been raised in the very closed Hebrew culture, it was a radical departure from the norm. John *had* to mention a gigantic detail like that. It was so mind-boggling that he couldn't conceive of leaving it out. But age and size differences were obvious. Everyone would have understood those details. From John's perspective, they would not have been worth mentioning. Yet, it seems obvious that they were present.

So, try to imagine what John saw. People of different generations—young and old alike. Various sizes—big and small, short and tall. Different cultures and ethnicities—"from *every* nation, from *all* tribes and peoples and languages." All of them worshiping together. That's the heavenly pattern.

The problem for us is that the average church here on Earth, especially the church in America, doesn't look like that. Most congregations are divided in every possible way. Typically, we gather with those who are culturally similar to ourselves, and, once we're in the building, we segregate further by ages and interests.

In my travels, I have encountered only a handful of churches that I would say are truly culturally diverse. According to sociologists, a congregation that is culturally/ethnically diverse is one that is comprised of no more than 80% of the members being from a single people group. To me, this definition seems to be a big stretch. To say that diversity could be four out of every five members all being of the same ethnicity doesn't really seem all that diverse, does it? Nevertheless, even using this broad definition, fewer than 6% of America's churches are truly diverse.[14]

In his article, "When Communers Become Consumers: Church Growth Rules That Could Be Making Your Church Sick," Greg Laurie said, "...some church-growth experts are telling pastors their 'customers' no longer attend to commune with God, but to 'consume' a personal or family service."[15] David M. Bailey expounded on Laurie's thoughts:

> "One consequence of our shift from 'communers' to 'consumers' is that the central attraction and focus of our communities are more on our preferences than on Jesus. Our communities tend to center on the preferences of our demographics.... The New Testament shows us that diversity of generations, social class, ethnicity, gender, and economic status within the local church community is important to God and His Body's life. However, we in the Body of Christ in America have devolved to such a state of dysfunctional division that we find it normal."[16]

Bailey is right. We are far separated from the heavenly pattern depicted in the book of Revelation, and, worse, we think we're okay.

Being together with different generations, economic classes, and ethnic backgrounds helps us to grow spiritually. Spending time with, and even worshiping with, people who are much older and much younger than us changes our perspective. Being among those who have more financial wealth than we do, as well as those who have less financial wealth, causes us to see from a different vantage point. Fellowshipping and worshiping with those from different cultural backgrounds helps us gain a more complete understanding of the *true* Body of Christ.

Too often, we have a tendency to "stick with our own kind." Right here in the United States, I have had the opportunity to minister in "Black" churches, "Chinese" churches, "Korean" churches, "Hispanic" churches, and more. And that's not to mention the many, many "White" churches who would never label themselves as such, but are, nevertheless.

Dividing like that impoverishes us. All we know is our own cultural perspective. We never—or rarely—get to see the Body of Christ in the larger context. What a shame.

Years ago, I was asked to help develop part of a curriculum about worship for use in various third-world countries. As I began to write many of the things I had taught for years, I realized how tainted my perspective was by my culture. So I tried to stretch my thinking to imagine how these ideas would translate in other cultures. When I did this, I recognized how limited I was in my understanding. Although the concepts I wrote were biblical in nature, they were limited by my life's experiences and my own cultural perspective. I'm guessing that you're likely in the same boat.

Those of us who are used to stoic, Anglo-Saxon churches in America have much to learn from the celebratory worship of many of our brothers and sisters in Africa. Similarly, those accustomed to the loud, exuberant, boisterous worship of places like South America or the Philippines, should be exposed to a more quiet and contemplative service. Those who insist on pipe organs as the sole instrument in worship would do well to regularly experience a guitar-based service. Likewise, those who believe that worship must have a full band—guitars, keyboards, bass, drums—should have the opportunity to be in an a cappella worship service.

If we recognize that worship is not about music presentation, or even the music itself, then we must realize that all of these issues are merely cultural. Experiencing a bit of each of those various cultures can help us see and know the fullness of worship in the whole Body of Christ. Doing this brings us closer to the heavenly pattern of worship.

GOING DEEPER

• Christ draws all manner of people unto Himself, and, when He is preeminent, the differences among us pale into insignificance. So, if we are overly distracted, or even offended, by how other people are different, what does this say about how much we have made Him preeminent in our hearts?

• The point isn't so much that diversity is good for us—although it is—as that it teaches us about God's heart, which embraces all sorts of people in all sorts of circumstances. When we consistently hang with a homogenous group—people just like us—could that say more about how connected we are with the Lord than about our tolerance, or lack thereof, for differences?

Worship in Heaven Is Loud

I know some people may be put off with the title of this chapter, but bear with me for a moment. You just might be challenged, like I was, as you consider this issue.

Recently, I spent some time at a retreat center. One afternoon, I was sitting on a dock on a small lake. Fifty yards or so away from me was a flock of geese frolicking on the shore. As I sat there, the geese started squawking, apparently because there were some people getting too close. Suddenly, though, their honking got noticeably louder. The volume increased considerably. I wondered why, but only for a second. As a pair of geese, wings outstretched, slowly glided downward from the sky, the geese on the shore looked skyward and squawked even more intensely.

My initial reaction was that this was a warning to intruders. Perhaps the translation was, "Stay away!" Actually—and you might find this hard to believe, but I'm not fluent in goose—I couldn't tell for sure.

I watched as the flying pair circled slowly around the small lake and descended even further. Then, just as I thought perhaps they might pull up and leave because of the noise, they landed in the water...right in front of the squawking group. I wondered if things would quickly turn ugly, with those who had already staked their claim fending off the trespassers, but I didn't have to wonder long. The two newcomers turned and swam right to the shore and joined the others.

Surprisingly, there was no testy confrontation. In fact, the others seemed to be welcoming them. It was then that I realized that these weren't uninvited guests at all. More likely, they were relatives, kinfolk, or at least long-lost friends. The raucous honking wasn't a warning; it was a greeting. "Hey, it's cousin Homer and his wife, Abigail!" "Welcome back, Homer!" "We're glad you're here!" (Again, not being fluent in contemporary goose language, I'm not entirely certain this is an accurate translation, but I think it's close.)

As I watched this scene unfold, I flashed back to a recent incident I encountered at an airport. I had just deplaned and was walking toward the security exit in the terminal concourse. Standing on the other side of security was a young man, perhaps in his early twenties. He was scanning, looking intently down the concourse, seemingly searching for someone. Just as I looked at him, his face suddenly lit up. He looked past me, waved his arms above his head, and, at the top of his voice, yelled, "Jessica!" He apparently had seen his beloved—perhaps wife or fiancée or girlfriend—and he was clearly excited about seeing her. He obviously didn't care that everyone else heard him calling, and we did hear him, because he was *really* loud. No, he wasn't the least bit concerned what anyone else thought, because he was excited about encountering the one he loved.

In both of the two Bible versions I use most frequently (the English Standard Version and the New International Version), the word "loud" is used twenty-one times in the book of Revelation. Contrast that with the single mention of "there was silence in heaven" (Revelation 8:1), and even that was only about a half hour. Apparently, quiet is the oddity in the heavenly realms. It should be noted, though, that the loudness is not electronically induced volume. There is no indication of any type of electronic amplification system. Nearly all of those twenty-one references are followed by the word "voice" or "voices." Even the relatively few references from Revelation we've looked at in this book so far have included these loud voices.

I would venture to say that, just like those geese and

just like the man at the airport, the folks in heaven are loud, not for the sake of making a lot of noise, but because they are excited. It's a fervent, intense outcry that is loud, not because the intended listener is hard of hearing, but because it is sparked by passion, emotion, and enthusiasm.

On the night of the most recent Super Bowl, after the game ended, a colleague posted on Facebook, "The loudest place in your town today...was it your AM service or was it the Super Bowl party afterward?" That's a thought-provoking question.

By asking this question, I am not emphatically suggesting that volume is the primary aim of our worship service. It isn't, nor should it be.[17] Note that clearly. However, decibel level among humans certainly corresponds to enthusiasm. If we're more vocal about a sporting event than we are about God, doesn't that tell us something about ourselves?

The loud voices we find in the book of Revelation are loud because of passion, a wholeheartedness. What they're shouting about is the greatness and majesty of God. Their voices are intense, because they're focused on things of eternal value, things that matter far more than football.

Perhaps we, too, should be loud in worship. Again, I am not suggesting raising the volume for the sake of being loud. No, the loudness should be the result of being excited, enthused, passionate. As we sing to and speak about the One Who has redeemed us, it should cause us to be energized and revived. That's the picture we see of worship in Heaven. Like that young man in the airport, we should be calling out, "Jesus!" Like the geese on the shore, our voices should reflect the intensity and excitement of the Lord, our God, Who visits us as we gather in His name.

I would suggest that our worship, in order to line up with the heavenly pattern, should be loud, but not loud just to make noise. I am certainly not suggesting raising the volume on the P.A. system or cranking up the guitar amp or the organ. Rather, it's a matter of giving full voice to what's in our heart. So, there should be—unless compelled by, say, communist oppression—no mumbling of words or half-voiced singing of songs. Any visitors to our worship services should immediately recognize our passion, when we worship. More than 250 years ago, John Wesley said it like this, "Sing lustily and with good courage. Beware of singing as if you were half dead, or half asleep; but lift up your voice with strength."[18]

I once saw a small church with a sign on the front door that read, "Silence prepares us for worship." Underneath the statement was a Bible reference, Habakkuk 2:20. That verse says, "But the Lord is in his holy temple; let all the earth keep silence before him." Years ago I heard the late Dr. Judson Cornwall comment on that passage, "That's in the Bible once, and I think we all ought to do it once." Of course, he smiled mischievously after he said it, but he made the point well. Undeniably, the vast majority of scriptural references to worship talk about things like singing and shouting and clapping. These are noisy activities that seem remarkably reminiscent of the worship we see depicted in John's Revelation.

Please realize that the people, angels, and creatures we see in the book of Revelation were not being loud to compete with one another in volume. There was no, "I can sing louder than you." It was not peer pressure to increase the noise level. Instead, volume appears to be a result of intensity, the outcome of being wholehearted.

Jesus said, "You shall love the Lord your God with all your heart and with all your soul and with all your mind and with all your strength" (Mark 12:30). To love God with all of our heart, soul, mind, and strength, seems to negate doing it halfway, doesn't it? There is simply no way to give something our all and simultaneously do it half-heartedly.

So, to be completely honest, I am not arguing so much for volume as I am for intensity and passion. Volume is simply the by-product of those. The geese I saw at the lake, the man I encountered at the airport, practically any serious fan at a sporting event, all of these and more attest to the fact that those who truly are intense about something, at some point will be loud about it.

Voice volume signifies intensity. No one, for example—except, perhaps in inane television commercials—shouts about things like their favorite brand of canned green beans or motor oil. Such things are boring, trivial, mundane to those of us who are not green bean or motor oil fanatics. They really don't warrant enthusiasm or zeal. It is only those things about which we are truly excited and passionate that cause us to raise our voices.

In light of this, is there—could there ever be—anything or anyone about which we should be more intense or passionate than the Lord and His mercy? No!!

I love the story about Jesus healing the ten lepers. He didn't cause their leprosy to immediately disappear while they were in front of Him. Instead, Jesus sent them on their way to the priests, so the priests could examine them to see that they had been healed. Then, Scripture declares, "As they went they were cleansed" (Luke 17:14). We don't know if they felt a tingling sensation, and, suddenly, the leprosy was gone. Or it is possible that one of them looked at one of the others and realized that his friend's leprosy had disappeared as they were walking. We're not given the details. We don't know how they figured it out. We just know they got healed while they were on their way to the priests.

My favorite part of this story, though, is not the healing itself, but the one guy who returned. "Then one of them, when he saw that he was healed, turned back, praising God with a loud voice" (Luke 17:15). One of the ten came back to thank Jesus. The Lord had miraculously healed him, and he wanted to give credit where credit was clearly due. Yet, he didn't slip quietly up to the side and give Jesus a timid, barely-noticeable thumbs-up. There was no half-smile with a slight head-nod. No, he was "praising God with a loud voice." He apparently wanted all to know what happened. Why? Because he had been instantly healed of a horrendous physical ailment. He wasn't going to be shy about such a pronouncement. God had intervened in a way that would alter the entire course of the rest of his life.

The fact of the matter is that you and I have had an encounter that was far greater. We have been healed of something much worse than leprosy. The sin that separated us from our Creator has been taken away, removed completely. It's gone forever! In light of this, how can we not be like that lone returning former leper and praise God with a loud voice? Let us, then, as Wesley said, "lift up your voice with strength"—like the inhabitants of Heaven—in worship to the Lamb on the throne, the Redeemer of our souls!

GOING DEEPER

- Do you ever find yourself, as Wesley put it, "singing as if you were half dead, or half asleep"? If so, what can you do to change this?
- We are commanded, "And you shall love the Lord your God with all your heart and with all your soul and with all your mind and with all your strength" (Mark 12:30). All that we are as persons is to be united in expressing our love and worship. How does this commandment relate to Tom's observation that worship in heaven is loud?
- Are you more enthusiastic at sporting events, or some other exhilarating activity, than you are about the Lord?

Worship in Heaven Is Demonstrative

A few years ago, I had the opportunity to preach for the first of three Sunday morning worship services at Oleviste Church in Tallinn, Estonia. With no official duties in the second service, I headed for the balcony to observe people from a different culture in worship. What I saw reminded me a bit of John's description of Heaven. An elderly man raised his hands. Moments later, a younger woman knelt down. My view of the service from the rear loft gave me a great vantage point. People all across the huge ancient cathedral were physically involved in expressing their worship to God. Although I could not understand their language, their physical expressions spoke volumes. To me, it was a little slice of Heaven.

The heavenly picture of worship from the Bible is not only passionate, but it is also demonstrative. The picture in Revelation is actually quite a compelling sight. The elders fall down and cast their crowns before the throne. The saints wave palm branches. Even the angels fall on their faces.

The worshipers are doing something. They are involved. There seems to be no indication of slouching posture or even of a rules-mandated standing at rigid attention. No, the participants seem to be engaging in such actions not out of coercion, but as a true response to God.

The frequent biblical references to physical expressions of worship are hard to miss. Especially in the book of Psalms, we are repeatedly told to do the very types of things we see happening in John's Revelation. Expressions like bowing and kneeling are frequent themes. Directives for raising hands, clapping hands, and even dancing(!) occur regularly in Scripture. Perhaps such commands help us better reflect the heavenly pattern of worship here on Earth.

The late Dr. Robert Webber was the most prolific author and teacher of the twentieth century on the subject of worship. In his audio series, *Worship Is a Verb,* Webber said, "Worship is not something that someone does *to* us. It is not something that someone does *for* us. But it is something done *by* us." He's right. Just like in the heavenly pattern, there is a necessary involvement—an outward demonstration—in worship.

The Bible includes many outward actions that are symbolic of inward realities. For example, people tore their clothes to indicate distress, perhaps over some calamity or disaster, or mourning a death, or even righteous indignation over sin. Although the tearing of garments was not commanded by God, it was an outward manifestation of something that was happening on the inside.

The Lord did, however, warn His people against such a sign that was only outward. In Joel 2:13, God said, "Rend your hearts and not your garments." They were apparently performing the outward sign apart from the inward reality, and the Lord told them to stop it.

In his New Testament letter, the Apostle James spends a great deal of time telling his readers that what is on the inside should be manifested on the outside. Over and over, James says that through our actions and our speech, there should be an outward demonstration of what God has done on the inside. The work God does in our hearts should become apparent to those with whom we interact.

The point, though, is not just to become like the Pharisees: whitewashed tombs. They looked good on the outside, but it was only on the outside. Their actions and words were definitely not a reflection of God's work on the inside. Actually, their hearts were not truly inclined toward God at all. Everything they did was just an outward show. Jesus confronted the hypocrisy of the Pharisees and even pointed it out to His disciples. He clearly wanted His followers to recognize such two-faced actions and to be on their guard against that. Unquestionably, what God is interested in is an outward demonstration of His work on the inside.

There are, of course, those who would say, "I'm just not a demonstrative person." Such people would suggest that standing with arms folded is a more accurate picture of who they are. It is more in line with their personality.

Well, the problem with such an idea is that personality is not all it's cracked up to be. For example, someone may say, "I can't help the way I act. I'm just not a kind and compassionate person." Guess what. The Bible says that followers of Christ should be kind and compassionate. So, does someone who is not innately kind and compassionate get a special pass to ignore that mandate? No! The fact is that, at that point, the person and God are incompatible...and God doesn't change.

Most Christians seem to understand this. We don't generally gloss over the areas in which we need to learn and grow. We repent and ask God to help us change. That's how we grow and mature. So why do we not do this with worship? For many people I've talked with over the years, it is almost as though the area of worship is off limits.

Of course, I realize that, because we are all different, we will never be exactly like one another. In fact, we shouldn't be. Even our worship should have some differences. That's a given. At the same time, though, left to our own sinful natures, we are all inclined toward the lowest common denominator. It is far easier to remain passive and uninvolved in worship (just like in most other areas of our Christian walk) than it is to actively engage, inwardly and outwardly.

Yet, we as leaders dare not allow this to happen. We should—just like in every other area of the Christian life—teach, encourage, and model where the rest of the flock should be heading. Where we see those who are reluctant to move forward, if we're truly good leaders, we must encourage such people and point them toward God's mercy and the Scriptures.

God's plan is to cause us all to mature in Him, both inwardly and outwardly. As we allow Him to work in our hearts, that work should become more and more evident in an outward way. This includes our worship.

Recently, I met a woman at one of our Worship Seminars. She told me that when she was young their family had a pet cardinal. The baby bird had apparently fallen from a nest and been abandoned by the mother. Their family took in the tiny cardinal and raised it as a pet.

The bird had one strange peculiarity, though. It didn't sing. Never. Wild cardinals outside the window sang, but this one didn't. The woman told me that one day she realized the reason. No one had ever taught it the song. No one around the bird knew the cardinal song, so it never learned to sing.

I think at least part of the problem with some people in the Church today is that they were never taught to be outwardly demonstrative in their worship. Because they never learned it, they're not sure how to do it. It seems foreign, uncomfortable, out of their comfort zones. Let's be honest, though. A lack of familiarity or comfort is not an adequate excuse to avoid biblical mandates.

Just because we've always been formal and stoic in church doesn't mean it's right. We've also been selfish and unforgiving at times. But the fact that we've been that way doesn't mean those actions are correct any more than having a stuffy attitude in church.

Prolific songwriter and pastor, Mark Altrogge, along with his son, Stephen, writes a blog. In a recent post entitled, "Men, Let's Worship Like Real Men," Stephen made these comments.

> "I want to issue a challenge to my fellow brothers (including myself): when we gather together on a Sunday morning to worship through song, let's worship like we really mean it. If you're in a church where there is hand raising, get your hands out of your pockets and lift them up to God. Sing your lungs out. Sing with unrestrained joy and a big smile on your face. Show your kids that real, macho men, don't give a rip what people think [about them] when it comes to worshiping God. Real men don't stand there impassively, arms crossed, barely mouthing the lyrics. Real men let it all hang out when it comes to worshiping God."[19]

Altrogge goes on to ask the question, "Why?" and answers it simply, "Because God is worthy."

The very next day, Stephen's dad, Mark Altrogge, wrote on a similar theme.

"If an outsider came into your Sunday meeting and observed you worshiping, what would he conclude you think about God?

"Does your expression of worship say how great and glorious, delightful and exciting you think God is? Does your worship say you've found God to be faithful and good, loving and satisfying? Would an outsider conclude you believe God to be real and present?

"Or does your worship say you find God about as exciting as an exam on protein chains (maybe you bio majors would get excited about this – I wouldn't). Do you sing with all the enthusiasm of someone who has just been asked to shovel 2 tons of manure? Does your worship say you believe God is distant and uncaring?

"What does our worship say about what God did for us? Do we sing like those who have been redeemed eternally from the wrath of God? Like those who have been seated with Christ in heavenly places? Like those who are grateful to have every sin wiped away? Do we rejoice like those who have the king of the universe living inside them?

"We should worship God expressively, not for a show or to impress others, but as a way of saying to him how much we love him. That we consider him to be infinitely great and glorious and majestic. That we consider him to be praiseworthy.

"Worship is primarily an issue of the heart. So

someone could worship God wholeheartedly and not show it on the outside. But I like what I once heard John Piper say – worship begins in the heart but should not stay there. It should be expressed."[20]

Years ago, I heard a statement that has stuck with me ever since. "As Christians, we do the most lying when we sing in church." It's true! We declare words about bowing before God or lifting our hands to Him, and all the while we neither bow nor lift our hands. Instead we stand upright with our arms folded stiffly in front of us. Hmmm. What's wrong with this picture?

Worship, if we are to truly reflect the heavenly pattern, will be demonstrative. Again, exactly what this looks like can vary—perhaps even vary greatly—from person to person. Not everyone will jump up and down or even wave their arms in the air. Some people will, by nature, be much more subdued than others. There should, however, be some outward demonstration of what God has done—and continues to do—in the heart. The idea that someone could regularly remain completely detached and non-participatory during worship clearly goes against the heavenly model we see in God's Word.

GOING DEEPER

- How would you answer Mark Altrogge's questions on page 77?
- How might our reluctance to witness to friends or colleagues be related to our reluctance to be demonstrative in worship?

SECTION 2

WHY DOESN'T WORSHIP ON EARTH RESEMBLE WORSHIP IN HEAVEN?

The World, the Flesh, and the Devil Compete for the Worship Due Only to God

We live in a fallen world. Sin has taken its toll on our planet...and on our lives. We also have an adversary who wants to devour us. And all of those things—the world, the flesh and the devil—compete for the worship that is due only to God.

The world

The world—our society in general, the media, the educational system, etc.—has stolen away the thinking of far too many Christians. Overall, the majority of those who are believers have been duped into wrong thinking by the world. Don't think so? Here are the facts.

- According to recent surveys, fewer than 10% of American Christians possess a truly biblical worldview. Just one out of ten!
- Only 40% said that they were absolutely committed to the Christian faith. This means that six out of ten Christians might be persuaded to try out something else.
- 62% of churched youth agreed with the statement: "Nothing can be known for certain except the things you experience in your life." Uhhh, excuse me for bringing this up, but what about the truth of the Bible?

I could go on with *many* other statistics, but I think you get the point. The mindset reflected in these statistics shows clearly that we, as believers, take too many of our cues from the world, rather than from Scripture. The world has usurped the thinking of far too many Christians.

A buddy of mine recently made a statement that struck me. A while back he had participated in Focus on the Family's, *The Truth Project*. In case you're not familiar with it, *The Truth Project* is a tremendous resource for helping to build a solidly biblical worldview. My friend commented that as he went through the course, he slowly became aware of how much of the world's system he had unknowingly bought into. Please realize that my friend and his family are good, godly people. If it can happen to them, it can happen to anyone. We all probably have too much worldly thinking inside us.

Likewise, due to modern communication and travel, we now have an unprecedented number of possible belief systems, and even "gods," all in close proximity to one another. If you live in or near a city of any significant size in the U.S., more likely than not there are people all around you who believe in a radically different way than you do about God and faith. They could be Muslim or Mormon, Buddhist or Baha'i, Hindu or Hare Krishna, Jewish or Jehovah's Witness, atheist or agnostic, and thousands of other possibilities. As we interact with such people on a regular basis, their perspectives, their worldviews, their ways of thinking, can begin to affect—and even, potentially, distort—our own ways of thinking.

My wife and I not only live together, but we also work together. Our ministry office is in our home. Sometimes, when I am working on a project on my computer, she will begin talking to me. Although, on some level, I am vaguely aware that she is speaking to me, at the same time, I am engrossed in the train of thought about what I am seeing on my computer screen. As a result, I miss most of what she said. (Please don't tell her this. She has no idea that I don't always give her my undivided attention.)

This same scenario can happen in our lives in a very different setting. We live and work in the world—in a worldly environment—for the entire week, and then go to our weekly Christian gatherings for worship. Yet our focus has been so absorbed in worldly things, so immersed in the things of Earth, that we can often miss the reality of God there in the worship service. We have to make a determined effort to pull away from a worldly and self-absorbed mindset. We must ask ourselves—and seek an honest answer to—the question, "Are we being shaped and formed by culture and media or by God's Word and the Gospel?"

I'll be the first to admit that this worldly pull can be a tricky thing to recognize in one's own life. It's sort of like asking a fish what it's like to live in water all the time. Even if the fish could talk, he would have no idea how to answer the question. It's his natural environment. He has never known anything different. We can have the same problem. Unlike the inhabitants of Heaven, living in the world is all we've ever known.

I can say this for sure, though. The more we allow God's Word to penetrate our thoughts, the more worldly thinking will be pushed out. Reading, studying, and memorizing Scripture on a frequent basis can help repel the mindset of the world and help us to be more conformed to the heavenly mindset.

The flesh

Added to the pull of the world is our own fleshly, sinful nature. Sin causes us to become self-absorbed. A colleague of mine suggests that many Christians—perhaps the majority?—have their internal radios tuned to WII-FM... What's In It For Me? This is even true when it comes to worship. Sin causes that to happen. We become more focused on us than on God.

Actually, our society practically forces us to focus on us and our little worlds. We view everything from our own perspectives. It all revolves around us. Of course, as Christians we would never actually admit that. We don't even really want to think such thoughts. It's not right to think such things, is it? We know that. Nevertheless, the truth can be seen in our actions.

Why do people today have five televisions in their homes, allowing each person to choose their own program? Why do so many families find it difficult to come to a consensus when trying to go out to eat? Each person wants their say in the matter. "We went to *his* choice last time!"

When I was a kid we had one television set. You watched what everyone else was watching or not at all. If we went out to eat, we didn't all get to vote. It wasn't that selfishness didn't exist when I was a kid. It did, just as much as it does now. But today, we seem to have given in to it. This everything-revolves-around-me mentality is pervasive in our society. It's everywhere. You see it repeatedly in the media. Movies, television shows, magazine advertisements, radio, billboards, social networking, computer games, and more, all reinforce it. It is nearly impossible to be unaffected by it. We get sucked into the mindset that everything is all about us.

For the majority of our lives, we control what we do. This is especially true for us as Americans. We do what we want when we want to do it. Don't interfere with our plans. We get into our cars and drive to whatever destinations we desire. When we have spare moments, we want to be entertained. Video games, television, surfing the net, or even shopping, are all ways of keeping ourselves amused during those moments when nothing in particular, nothing of significance, is happening.

In stark contrast, in a reference to our worship of God in a congregational setting, John Jefferson Davis said, "This is not like driving my car; I am not in control; I will go where God wants to take me; this is not a trip to the mall; this is not about 'consumption,' this is not about 'entertainment,' but about the praise and presence of God—the God who is more lastingly real than the car in which I drove to get here."[21] I like that. Jefferson hit the nail on the head. Especially in the area of worship, we need to get over the I-Me-Mine mentality caused by our fleshly natures and shift our focus to God, the ultimate reality.

Not long ago, an acquaintance of mine posted an amazing quote on Facebook. He cited it as being from an anonymous source, but it is definitely worth pondering. "It is functional blasphemy to stand in the place of God. God is the audience of worship. If we become the audience it is blasphemy."[22] I think that's accurate: functional blasphemy. I know I don't want to—and I'm pretty sure you don't want to—be guilty of blasphemy. Yet, even in congregational worship, we can too easily shift the main focus to us, can't we?

Too much focus on me—my needs, wants, and desires—and I become too large in my own mind. When that happens, a corresponding opposite reaction also results. If I have become greater, whether intentionally or not,

God becomes smaller. My great self crowds Him out.

Try this. Stop reading, and stare intently for a few moments at an object across the room from you. As you gaze at it, you are aware of other objects in the range of your peripheral vision. Those objects, though, are blurry, out of focus. The one object that is in focus is clear and distinct. Even if that object is relatively smaller than other things around it, that is still the one object that is the point of focus. As worshipers, we need a focus shift at the deepest levels, off of us and onto God.

If God really is as great, vast, and overwhelmingly wonderful as we declare, then can we willingly allow such trivial things to consistently pull our attention away from Him? I think not. Don't allow your fleshly, sinful nature to cause you to miss that God—and He only—should be the focus in our worship.

The devil

Finally, we have an enemy who tries to distract our attention from the Lord. When Satan tempted Jesus in the wilderness, he tried to get the Savior away from giving all glory to God. Satan somehow showed Jesus all the kingdoms of the world and promised to give them to Him, if only Jesus would bow down and worship him. Jesus knew, though, that as dazzling as the things of Earth may appear, they are no match for the one true God.

Satan hasn't really changed. He still does not want the people of God to worship the Lord Almighty. So, he will put distractions and roadblocks in our paths to keep us from doing that. Here is one simple example to which just about everyone can relate: Have you ever had serious problems getting ready for, or getting to, a church service? Why does it appear that, so frequently, Sunday morning is the time when everything seems to go wrong?

I could share stories of Sunday morning mishaps from my own life, as well as countless others I've heard as I travel. In reality, though, those stories would only be anecdotal information. They would be just subjective bits of data that would not truly add any objective arguments to my overall case. Yet the sheer volume of them—story after story after story—makes me think there actually is some commonality to such accounts. After all, what non-Christians have you ever met who have so consistently encountered obstacles on the way to the coffee shop on Sunday mornings? I would venture to say that they would be few and far between. Why is that? Because the enemy of our souls doesn't care in the least about whether or not you, or anyone else, goes and buys coffee. A Christian going to church, on the other hand, presents a problem for him. The demonic world does not want us to worship God.

Ephesians 6:12 tells us, "For we do not wrestle against flesh and blood, but against the rulers, against the authorities, against the cosmic powers over this present darkness, against the spiritual forces of evil in the heavenly places." Anyone who would suggest there is no spiritual opposition isn't reading the Bible. We have an enemy who opposes us—especially to prevent us from worshiping God—but that doesn't mean we should just accept it. The preceding verse in Ephesians 6 says that we should stand against the schemes of the devil.

Satan will try any means necessary to keep us from worshiping God. Temptations. Distractions. Misunderstandings. Discouragements. Mishaps. Relational issues. And so many other possibilities, but all with one goal: to keep our eyes off of God. We need, as Ephesians 6:11 tells us, to stand against our enemy's schemes.

Do we just let it happen?

The world, our sinful nature, and the devil—the unholy trinity—work in grotesque harmony to frustrate our attempts to worship God. With a trio of such formidable opponents, it is no wonder, then, that our worship here on Earth looks considerably different than the picture of worship from the book of Revelation. So what do we do?

Well, once we recognize this opposition, it is then up to us whether we willingly allow it to happen. Don't misunderstand. There is no indication in Scripture that, this side of Heaven, we will ever be completely adversary-free. The world, the flesh, and the devil will be nipping at our heels until the day we graduate to Glory. However, once we recognize the battle, we must then make the choice as to whether we simply give up and let them win, or we fight back. I hope you find the idea of rolling over and playing dead as distasteful as I do. But unless we make the effort to push back, we are, in essence, giving up. When we refuse to take action in those areas where we see the world and its ideals creeping into our lives, we are giving up the fight. If we willingly allow our selfish nature, to keep undermining our efforts at worship—personal and/or congregational—we are throwing in the towel. If we give up when we encounter obstacles to our worship, then our enemy wins.

If the worship of God truly is—as Christians for centuries have declared—our highest priority, then whatever may detract from that worship must be pushed aside. Worship of Almighty God is worth the effort. Fight the good fight. Don't let those opponents interfere with your worship of the King. Instead, you and I should do everything possible to emulate the worship we see depicted in the heavenly realms.

GOING DEEPER

- Are you truly being shaped and formed by culture and media or by God's Word and the Gospel?
- In what areas of your thinking and behaving do you suspect you may not be thoroughly in line with Scripture? How do you feel about your answer? Is there something you should consider changing as a result of your answer?
- What is blasphemy? Put into your own words what is meant by "it is functional blasphemy...if we become the audience of worship."
- What are some of the ways the devil tries to drive wedges between you and the Father?

We Have a Compartmentalized View of Life

As if our many *real* activities don't keep our hearts and minds divided enough, most people in our culture, Christians included, live in several alternate realities simultaneously. The entertainment industry provides us with a seemingly endless array of possibilities. There are, for our pleasure, movies and television, live theater and concerts, music-to-go on an mp3 player, electronic games that can whisk us away to another place or even another time. There are a plethora of choices that can take us away from our everyday lives. What I'm about to say may not be popular with some people, but it is true, nevertheless. The more we engage in such experiences, the more the boundaries get blurred between the real and the imaginary.

Today, in our western society, we live overly-compartmentalized lives. You can be an online gaming champion on Saturday, a football fan on Sunday, a businessman on Monday, a soccer coach Monday night, a virtual softball shortstop on Tuesday night, a Guitar-Hero champion on Wednesday morning, president of the Horticultural Society on Thursday night, and so on. In times past, such a panoply of options did not exist. Now, we have more opportunities to be involved in more activities than our grandparents ever even imagined possible. Oftentimes, these segmented compartments don't overlap in our minds. Each one is completely separate. With a track record of having these various separated facets of our lives, it is easy to do the same thing with our spiritual lives. Sunday morning becomes the time for God, with no further thought given to Him until the next Sunday.

More and more people in our society see these illusory experiences as true realities. They spend an increasingly larger amount of time in such virtual realities and less time in the "real" world. As a result, they begin to see everything in that context: separate little worlds that don't need to connect to one another. So, for example, if you go to church, that's fine...for you. But if your "churchy" ideas start to invade other areas of your life, such people don't understand. To them, it would be the same as their online World of Warcraft experience affecting their eating lunch. Those are totally separate; one has nothing to do with the other.

Yet, the truth is that no one experience in our lives stands in isolation from the rest. Especially, as those who have been made whole and complete in Christ, the notion of having separate compartmentalized areas inside of us is incorrect thinking. All areas of life impact all other areas. The effect may be small, or it could be large, but it all ties together, somehow.

I remember many years ago playing—incessantly—a popular new video game called Tetris. In case you don't know, Tetris is a game where different colored blocks (squares, rectangles, L-shapes) drop randomly from the top of the screen. The player must maneuver the blocks to fit in perfectly to the ones that have reached the bottom. You stack the blocks and attempt to leave no extra space between blocks. If you fill a certain number of rows with the blocks and leave no empty holes, you go on to the next level. As I said, I played this game a lot. It never occurred to me that playing a silly computer game might somehow be detrimental to my worship. Yet one Sunday morning at church, when I closed my eyes during a time of worship, I saw colored blocks dropping down. Instead of having my mind focused on Christ, I was back at my computer seeing those seemingly innocuous boxes falling. I knew I had played Tetris too much and needed to make a change.

Added to the imaginary "realities" is the fact that we are constantly bombarded with the notion that the material world is the ultimate reality. When this happens, our view of God diminishes. At the very least, we will subconsciously divide everything into two distinct categories. There is the natural world and the supernatural. Of course, as followers of Christ, we will verbally declare that the supernatural world is the most important. Yet, if we're honest, the majority of our attention is usually focused on the natural world. That which we can readily see, hear, feel, taste, and smell takes center stage. The "supernatural"—the arena of God, faith, prayer, worship, etc.—gets shoved to the side.

Allow me a moment to demonstrate this. Let's say you were to receive a promotion at work. What would be your first reaction? Would you revel in the effort you've put forth—the long hours, the creativity and diligence? Would you congratulate yourself for taking the initiative of furthering your education? Would you pull out your phone to inform family and friends about the good news? All of these would be likely first choice scenarios, right? But would you—as an initial response—humbly bow your head and thank the One Who has granted you the ability and talents in the first place? Your *very first* reaction?

How about this scenario. When faced with an illness—large or small—the first response of most Christians is not to "take it to the Lord in prayer." Instead, our initial response is to call or see a physician. Don't misunderstand my meaning here. I am keenly aware that God often works through doctors. Yet, if our *first thoughts* are not toward the ultimate Healer, perhaps we, too, have bought into the notion that there are two distinct segments of reality, and, worse, that the natural world trumps the supernatural. In practice, we give too much credence to the one we *say* is secondary.

The truth is that such a dichotomy between the natural and supernatural is erroneous. God made it all. There is a cohesiveness, a completeness, in the whole of creation that is lost when we separate the visible from the invisible. Too much of a focus on that which is seen leaves the unseen neglected, and, therefore, diminished in our lives.

The idea of separating one from the other—the physical world from the spiritual one—has been present throughout history, but it has been brought strongly to the forefront by modern scientific thinking. The "modern" age and its scientific discoveries have benefited mankind in a myriad of ways. Yet, such benefits are not without corresponding perils. As our goods and wealth abundantly increase, it is easy to forget the God who has given us such things.

The ability to "live" in so many worlds simultaneously, while most of the time ignoring the God who causes all of those things to be in harmony with one another, can push aside our overarching purpose to glorify the Lord in *all* we do. Living compartmentalized lives, where everything we do is disconnected from everything else, can cause us to miss the reality of God in those various areas.

So what do we do? We need to make a point of recognizing life as a whole. If there are segments of your life that seem to be disconnected from everything else, maybe it's time to evaluate the validity of those things. Make a point to put God first in each area of your life to honor Him. That's really the point of worship, right? When we do this, then our times of corporate worship will have more of the sense of the full and complete worship we see in the heavenly model of worship.

GOING DEEPER

- The enemy's primary tool for driving wedges between us and the Father is deception or lies about what is really true or really important. What do you think is the main difference between what a world under the devil's dominion considers to be really true or important and what God says is really true or important?
- If we have all these compartments in our lives, is the best way to improve our spiritual health simply to make sure God has the biggest compartment? What do you think is the best way to bring sanity to lives in which we have to function in so many different arenas?
- In what area of your life do you find the greatest struggle relinquishing full control to God?

We Have an Incorrect Focus

Recently, I mounted a scope on my .22-caliber rifle. (No, I'm not really a hunter. It's more of a sportsman hobby.) After following the instructions for mounting the scope, I took it outside to sight it in. I shot, and made the necessary adjustments after each shot. It got closer and closer with each adjustment. After fifteen minutes, I thought that it was as good as it was going to get. I am, after all, not that great a marksman. Then I noticed that the scope had come loose a bit. I had to take it off the rifle and remount it. Then the sighting-in process began again.

I did notice that when the focus was off—not accurate—then the shot was also off. That may seem obvious, but I think there's a lesson here for us about worship. If our focus is misaligned, our worship will be off, too.

It should be understood that the snapshots we viewed of Heaven's worship from Revelation are more than just some nice thoughts written to give us something to which we can look forward someday. Indeed they are that, but they can also help serve as patterns for us here and now, pushing us to line up our actions more and more with the activity of Heaven.

I've seen and experienced worship here on Earth in many settings. I've been in worship services in dozens of different denominations, even in other nations and with various ethnic groups. Black Pentecostal churches where shouting and dancing were the norm. Staid—even stoic—high-church settings, with lots of formalism. Laid back, unceremonious blue-jeans-and-bare-feet, grab-yourself-a-cup-of-coffee services. Even a few churches that truly are multicultural, not just claiming to be. I've pretty much seen every earthly expression of worship. Reading the glimpses of worship in Heaven, though, challenges my understanding of true worship. The wholehearted, unashamed, singularly-fixed worship before the throne gives me pause. I begin to wonder if I have ever seen worship expressed so freely, so unabashedly. To my shame, I am certain that *I* have never expressed worship in such a selfless manner myself.

Oftentimes, our worship here and now is characterized by lackadaisical attitudes. There is little passion or enthusiasm. Most of us spend more time thinking about our comfort, rather than about the Object of our worship, the Lord Himself.

Long before he reached the zenith of his notoriety, the late Dr. Robert Webber wrote an article entitled, "Let's Put *Worship* into the Worship Service." In the article he made a great statement.

> "False approaches to worship perturbed the Reformers. The medieval church had taken worship away from the people and located it in the work of the celebrants and choir. Everyone else watched as if they were at a play. A monumental achievement of the Reformers was to give worship back to the people. Now we have come full circle. Worship no longer belongs to the people. It has become something someone does for us.... But the Bible understands worship as God-centered... It is time to turn our backs on substitutes for real worship and learn what it means to be a people who truly worship God."[23]

Those words, now penned nearly thirty years ago, sound almost prophetic for this hour. When we—our preferences, our likes, our wants—become the focus of worship, we have taken gigantic strides away from the worship of Heaven. Such thoughts are nowhere close to what we see in John's Revelation. There is no indication that any of them stopped, folded their arms, and refused to participate because the words were unusual or the melody uncomfortable. Honestly, in the context of Heaven's worship, such an idea seems ludicrous. We would find a scenario like that impossible to even imagine, yet it happens here on a regular basis. Perhaps there is something misaligned in the focus of our earthly worship, something that is present—and even fundamental—in the worship of Heaven.

There is, indeed: a singular fixation on Who God is and what He's done.

Read through some of the words of worship in the opening story again. Look at them closely. Ask yourself, "What is the focus?" Is it about the worshipers or the One being worshiped?

By the way, the easiest way to recognize this is by determining who or what is driving the verbs in the sentences. For example, suppose I say, "I worship You, Lord." Although that statement is addressed *to* God, it is not really *about* God. It is about me and what I am doing. "*I* worship..." Similarly, something along the lines of, "Forever, we will honor You," is also about us and what we will do. We may be addressing God in these statements, but what we will do is the main thrust of the statements. In both of these examples, the verbs are being set in motion by us. It is our actions—not the Lord—that is really the focus in what we are saying.

Please understand that I am not suggesting that using such words is definitely and emphatically wrong. I am, however, suggesting that the heavenly picture does not offer such a pattern. Words that are about *us* and what *we* do fit well into a society where the focus has become us. However, we dare not remove the Lord as the focal point in the Church. If we do so, then our worship has become, in reality, no different than the worship of any other religion: focused on what I get from God and what I do, with little or no thought given to Who He is and what He's done, giving Him the glory that is truly due His Name.

So, with that understanding in mind, take a look once more at the words from our heavenly pictures.

> "Holy, holy, holy is the Lord God, the Almighty—the One who always was, who is, and who is still to come."[1]

> "You are worthy, O Lord our God, to receive glory and honor and power. For you created all things, and they exist because you created what you pleased."[2]

> "Worthy are you to take the scroll and to open its seals, for you were slain, and by your blood you ransomed people for God from every tribe and language and people and nation, and you have made them a kingdom and priests to our God, and they shall reign on the earth."[5]

> "Worthy is the Lamb Who was slaughtered—to receive power and riches and wisdom and strength and honor and glory and blessing."[6]

> "Blessing and honor and glory and power be to Him who sits on the throne, and to the Lamb, forever and ever!"[7]

> "Salvation comes from our God who sits on the throne and from the Lamb!"[8]

> "Amen! Blessing and glory and wisdom and thanksgiving and honor and power and might be to our God forever and ever! Amen."[11]

With the exception of the very last part of Revelation 5:10 ("and they shall reign on the earth"), those words offer a single focus: the Lord—Who He is and what He has done. Even the "they shall reign" portion stems from what God has done. Further, the ones saying those "they shall reign" words are not the ones about whom the words are spoken. No, there is no self-acknowledging in this scene at all. In other words, it's not about me. It's all about the Lord—Who He is and what He has done.

Perhaps, just as important as the words that *are* said, would be the words that are *not* said. I see no indication of, "Lord, *we* bow before You." Or, "God Almighty, *we* lay our crowns at Your feet." Those myriad of worshipers are not speaking about themselves. There is no—whether blatant or subtle—"Hey, look at me." The focus, from beginning to end, is exclusively on God.

Several times over the years, I have heard preachers ask the question, "Isn't it amazing what a prayer can do?" Actually, the answer to that question is, "No." Prayer can't do anything. It is the God to Whom the prayer is directed Who does it all. To suggest that prayer is amazing would be like a man who, when asked about his employment, which he loves, instead tells about his car that he drives to get to his workplace. "It gets great gas mileage, but it still has plenty of room for me to be able to carpool. The acceleration is amazing. And did I mention the safety rating? It's got..." He goes on and on about the transportation *to* the job, and misses telling *about* the job. Yet the car is only the vehicle that gets him there, just like prayer is not the end; it's only the vehicle.

Similarly, to talk about us worshiping as though that is the major point is actually to miss the main point. When our songs declare, "*I* worship You," then we're not actually doing what we're talking about. The focus is on me and my "worship," when the focus should be on God.

C.S. Lewis said it like this, "The perfect church service, would be one we were almost unaware of. Our attention would have been on God. But every novelty prevents this. It fixes our attention on the service itself; and *thinking about worship is a different thing from worshipping*."[24] Lewis is right.

I recently read an article for worship leaders on the internet. In one section the writer talked about the overemphasis of music in worship. One sentence in particular struck me. "The focus of *worship*, however is not the music, but the worship." Actually, that, too, misses the point. The focus of our worship should never be the worship itself; it should always be God.

I see this as the most significant difference between the worship in Heaven, as depicted in John's Revelation, and the worship by the Church on Earth, especially the American Church: we too frequently miss what should be the true focus of our worship.

Please recognize that I am aware that Psalms and other sections of Scripture sometimes have an emphasis on the worshiper (as opposed to the One being worshiped), so, again, I am not suggesting that such phraseology is emphatically incorrect or blatantly wrong. Instead, I am attempting to offer a much needed balance. Too much of what is said and sung in the Church today is about us. The focus is too frequently on you and me. Christian singer/songwriter Scott Wesley Brown said, "Worship this side of Heaven is held hostage to our own personal experiences, traditions, imaginations and devices..." [25] This may be partly because of our culture, or it may be simply because of our sinful nature. Whatever the cause, I am suggesting that we should purposely work to shift the emphasis away from us and, instead, direct it toward God.

I am not saying that songs that are not God-directed are emphatically wrong to sing congregationally. Some songs speak of God's love for us, His goodness toward us, or His promises for us. These are good things, and they can cause our hearts and minds to be turned toward Him in worship. Ultimately, though, our focus must be primarily on the Lord Himself. Otherwise, we can't truly call what we're doing worship. We may be singing good, meaningful, and even heartfelt songs, but if the focus is on anything but the Lord Himself, it's not worship. Again, this does not mean that singing such songs is wrong. They might be perfect for a particular service. Just recognize that if God is not the focal point, then what we're doing is not really worship.[26]

In a recent article in *Worship Leader* magazine, James MacDonald, pastor of Harvest Bible Chapel in Chicago, made a similar observation. Here is a short excerpt.

> "I'm not seeking to parse meanings with undue rigor, but we need to be precise in our definitions if we want to accurately embrace the very purpose for our existence. Worship is the actual act of ascribing worth directly to God. Worshipful actions [earlier in the article he mentions things like acts of kindness and generosity toward others, for example] may do this indirectly, but when the Bible commands and commends worship as our highest expression, it is not talking about anything other than direct, intentional, vertical outpouring of adoration. While that does not have to be put to music, it does have to be direct in order to rise above the 'worshipful' and actually attribute worth to God...."[27]

In an article entitled, "Why Worship Means Nothing," popular blogger and worship leader Kim Gentes recently shared a similar conclusion.

> "For a moment, let's roll back the clock 40 years. If you were to ask a linguist, scholar and Bible trans-

> lator what the word 'worship' meant, according to the Biblical usage of it, you would get something akin to 'pointed acts and moments of submission, sacrifice and obeisance.' But today, the worship word has become almost a euphemism for 'everything.' This has happened not because the Bible changed, but because we stopped using it as the central text to define the word. And with the popular worship movement of the last 30 years, we have co-opted the 'worship' term for almost everything and anything to which that movement was associated. I have done it, others have done, we've all done it. But we were wrong."[28]

Although they came at the subject from very different perspectives, I think both MacDonald's and Gentes' statements are right on target. Worship is directed toward God. If He isn't the focus, then it can't truly be called worship.

Oftentimes, the problem of incorrect focus is compounded by those in leadership. In a corporate worship setting, leaders can inadvertently send the wrong message. The décor and accoutrements can send unintentional, inappropriate signals to those who attend our churches. Cushy chairs, theater-style seating, bright spotlights on the platform area can all contribute to an enjoy-the-show atmosphere. This can—not intentionally, perhaps, but no less in reality—draw the attention away from the One who has promised to be present and Who we are there to worship.

One of my sons recently attended a Christian conference. During a time of worship, the "house" lights dimmed and colored spotlights illuminated the musicians up front. The leader began by saying, "We don't want you to view this as a show..."

My son, sitting in the congregation, thought, *If you don't want us to view this as a show, then why the colored lights?* He's got a point.

Please understand that this is not a generational difference. My son is just twenty-two years old. He's not an old guy like me, but he does recognize that the point of worship is to focus on God, not us.

As we discussed this experience, my son made another tremendous observation. This obviously was not the first time he was in a setting where the main lights were dimmed for worship. He expressed that it seemed odd, since there won't be any darkness in Heaven. So, for people who have always been in churches where the lights are dimmed for worship, Heaven will seem even more foreign to them than it will to the rest of us. Another great point.

Maybe for all our talk of not making worship a show, often it has become one, anyway. Perhaps it would be good to remove the emphasis from the people in the front, and, instead, direct our attention toward God. A.W Tozer said this, "A church that can't worship must be entertained; and men who can't lead a church to worship must provide entertainment."[29] Although Tozer made this statement more than fifty years ago, his words sound ominously appropriate for today. If all we've got is a "kickin'" band and some pretty lights, we may as well pack up and go home. The world can offer those things.

More recently, Scott Wesley Brown made a great comment. "A worship leader is a doorman in the master's house. He is not there to entertain the guests with himself, but to take them to the master!"[30] That's not just a nice, pious-sounding observation; it's true. If the leadership isn't primarily pointing people toward God, they're not truly helping the people to worship.

As I travel, I am often asked about topics like lowering the brightness of the room lighting while increasing the lighting on the platform. In all honesty, the dimmed houselights with floodlights on the platform can help create a "safe" environment, where people are less concerned about others around them. More commonly, though, it offers great potential for nonparticipation. Nobody's watching, so I can do what I want. More importantly, I don't have to do what I don't feel like doing right now: actively engaging in worship.

Although we were created to worship God, our fleshly nature fights against it. Offering an atmosphere of noninvolvement makes it easier for people to opt out.

Worship leaders frequently ask me, "How do we get our people to participate more in the worship service?" Unless the question is asked in a public setting (where I don't really want to embarrass or humiliate them), my response is generally a series of questions:

- Do you dim the house lights when the music

starts?

• Does the lighting on the platform create a show-like atmosphere?

• Do you run the sound so loud that people can't hear themselves sing?

• Do you do lots of new and difficult songs?

Generally, they answer in the affirmative to most or all of these questions. I then simply follow up by asking, "And you're wondering why people aren't participating?" I don't think this is rocket science.

Not long ago I visited a church on Sunday morning. To say that they had technical difficulties during worship that morning would be an understatement. The vocals and the worship leader's guitar seemed to be cutting in and out of the sound system. It went from blaring to non-existent and back to blaring. One of the sound techs had hurried to the platform to try to straighten things out. It was one of those worship-leader-nightmare scenarios. Having led congregational worship more than a thousand times, I recognized this as one of those situations you hope will never happen to you, but at some point it does.

In this particular setting, I was actually stunned by the response of the congregation. They barely missed a beat. One of the pastors stepped up and asked people to speak out their praises to God. One person after another spoke exaltation to the Lord: His greatness, His goodness, His mercy, His majesty, His holiness, His faithfulness, on and on they went. No singing, but worship nevertheless. The congregation paid little attention to the frantic attempts to get the sound system functioning correctly. Their gaze was fixed on the King.

I had to wonder how few churches would have been able to keep such a service from simply falling apart. In most congregations, the people would have been so totally consumed with the problems that they would have been distracted from the real point: worshiping God. Perhaps we've trained people to be so utterly dependent on someone leading the worship that we can't worship without that. Yet it seems to me that in Heaven, no one is leading. Such leadership is unnecessary. Why? Because when your focus is fixed on Him, nothing else matters. Potential distractions are not disruptive. Everything else pales in comparison.

This is not to say that we should get rid of those who lead in worship. Again, there is a qualitative difference between Earth and Heaven. We are easily distracted here and now. It is good to have someone who helps us focus our attention on God. At the service I just mentioned, one of the pastors stepped up and invited the people to voice their own praises to God. His quick actions helped keep the focus where it rightfully belonged. As God's people, we should be learning more and more to fix our eyes on Him. We should worship Him in spite of anything else going on around us.

We need to return our focus to the Object of our worship, Almighty God. The other things—the peripherals—are not really all that important. They can have value, but that value should never be seen on the same level as—or even close to the same level as—the Lord Himself. If He is not the singular main focus of our worship, then clearly something is wrong.

GOING DEEPER

- If you were to start everything you think and do with a consideration of what it will be like in heaven, how do you think this might change your life? Answer in concrete, specific, and practical ways.
- Describe what a difference it makes for you when you know that God is your focus in worship, rather than your own experience of worship being the focus.
- If worship in your church is structured in any of the ways described here as potential distractions from keeping your focus on God, what are they? What can you do—and will you do—to keep your proper focus and not be distracted by these things?

We Have an Incorrect Perception of God

Most Christians in our culture have a grossly distorted perception of God. Because we spend so much time in the center of everything, we see God as only a larger—lots larger, of course—version of ourselves. If something bad happens to us, we picture God as vengeful and mean. If something exceptionally positive occurs, we think of Him as kind and good-hearted. Yet, if we really knew Him *as He is*, it would change our approach to worship.

In Heaven, our knowing of God will be complete and full. That's not true here and now. There, we'll know

Him as He is; we'll see Him face to face. Here and now we don't have that privilege.

While we are on Earth, our knowing of God comes primarily from His Word. It is what He has objectively revealed about Himself. Of course, we can know some things about God from other sources, like nature, beauty, emotions, and other people, for example, but those are subjective. The objective truth of His Word gives us the most complete and accurate picture we will have here on Earth. The fact is, the more we know God through His Word, the more complete our worship will be, and our worship here will become more and more like the worship of Heaven.

I recently got what is commonly called a smart phone. I knew beforehand that it had some amazing capabilities. The more I use it, however, the more astounded I am by the technology. Of course, I can use it for making calls, texting, and taking pictures, just like my previous phone, but that's only a small fraction of its potential. I can, in a matter of seconds, check the weather...anywhere on the planet. Additionally, I can not only see if my next flight is on time, I can check in for that flight and have my boarding pass sent to my phone so I don't need to keep track of another piece of paper. I can play music, look at photos, browse the internet, check the latest news, keep my ongoing schedule, and even use it to wake up in the morning. And I'm still only skimming the surface of what it can do. Scanning barcodes to look up the best place to buy a particular item is a pretty handy feature. I also have an app that turns my phone into a guitar tuner. Plus, there's a guitar chord finder that allows me to input practically any chord name, and it shows me how to play that chord on the guitar. I can even play piano and drums right on the phone. The more I get to know about and understand this electronic marvel, the more I am amazed at it.

My wife and I have been married for more than thirty years. In ways similar to my increasing marvel at my smart phone, the longer my wife and I are together, the more I love her. I understand her more. I know her better. Some of the things that originally attracted me to her are now enhanced, because I've seen those things in action for so long.

All of that to say this: In order to worship God fully, we need to know Him, to know who He is. More than just having a superficial understanding that He's our Friend in the sky, we need to be more and more grasping the fullness of Who He is. Why? Because the more we truly know Him—and I'm talking about knowing Him *as He really is*, not just the way we'd like Him to be—the more we will worship Him.

Because God has revealed Himself in Scripture, it seems obvious, then, that meditation on Scripture should be a major part of what drives us to worship. Beholding God—Who He is and what He's done—from His Word will cause our hearts and minds to be turned toward Him in worship.

Author and pastor, Glenn Packiam, said that, too frequently today, people who are planning corporate worship services "begin by asking, 'What's in my heart?'

instead of 'What's true about God?' But worshiping authentically is not the same as worshiping in Truth. One has to do with being heartfelt; the other with being correct."[31] He's right. The revealed truth of His Word absolutely must be the undergirding that guides and shapes our worship here on Earth.

A passage that seems reminiscent of the sections from Revelation on which my opening story is based is found in Isaiah 6. Isaiah saw the Lord high and lifted up, and there were seraphim—great angels—there in the scene. They each had six wings, but they only used two for flying. The others they used for covering their faces and feet. Have you ever wondered why they did that? That seems strange, doesn't it?

Is it possible that it was out of a sense of modesty on their part and a reverence toward God? Don't misunderstand. These were great and mighty creatures, but compared with God, they weren't in the same league. They weren't even second class. No, compared to the Lord Most High, they would have been more like forty-seven trillionth class. Standing before Him, they would have recognized that fact. Perhaps covering face and feet was the only logical course of action. They would not have been embarrassed, yet they could easily have had a strong sense of not measuring up to the One on the throne. When placed in juxtaposition with the Creator of all, they likely could have realized, "He's God...and I'm definitely not."

A.W. Tozer said it this way, "We can't worship these

days because we do not have a high enough opinion of God. God has been reduced, modified, edited, changed and amended until He is not the God Isaiah saw high and lifted up but something else."[32] Tozer went on to add these thoughts, "Christ can never be known without a sense of awe and fear accompanying the knowledge. He is the fairest among ten thousand, but He is also the Lord high and mighty. He is the friend of sinners, but He is also the terror of devils. He is meek and lowly in heart, but He is also Lord and Christ who will surely come to be the Judge of all men. No one who knows Him intimately can ever be flippant in His presence."[33] Tozer is exactly right.

Habituation is a psychology term that refers to our amazement about something fading over time. As we become accustomed to whatever it is, the thing that once amazed us becomes ordinary, mundane. It's the reason that couples seem to "fall out of love." The unfortunate reality is that we can too readily do this with the Lord. We become accustomed to Him and no longer reverence Him.

The truth is that in our culture today, we have emasculated God. Any sense of mystery and wonder has been lost, yet God is far greater than we can imagine. And, unlike my smart phone—or even my wife—God is limitless. We will never plumb the depths of what He is like.

Let me take you on a brief imaginative journey. Let's say that next weekend at your church, you're worshiping in the midst of the congregation, when suddenly you hear a loud, clear voice booming through the sanctuary. It reminds you of thunder, or, perhaps, the crashing of the ocean's waves. Of course, being the curious type—and wondering what on Earth is making all that noise—you turn to see. But no matter what you might have thought was behind you, you could never have expected what you see. You encounter something like a man, but whose face is blazing like the sun, so bright you are forced to shield your eyes with your hand. Even in the midst of the brilliant light, you can still see that He has distinct eyes of fire, flashing and piercing. Out of His mouth comes a sharp two-edged sword. His hair is a brilliant blizzard of white, and He is dressed in a long, dazzlingly white robe with a gold breastplate that gleams. Then, from the midst of that cacophony of sights and sensations, He speaks, boldly and forcefully, "I am First, I am Last, I'm Alive. I died, but I came to life, and my life is now forever. See these keys in my hand? They open and lock Death's doors, they open and lock Hell's gates."[34]

I encourage you, right now, right where you're at, to close your eyes and try to picture this scene. See the risen Christ in His resplendent glory. See His face blazing like the sun, and hear His voice speaking loudly, but kindly, to you. If this really happened—if the scene I portrayed above really occurred at your church this weekend—how would you respond? I'm pretty sure that you or I encountering such a scene would likely react much like the Apostle John did when he saw the Lord like this. "When I saw him, I fell at his feet as if I were dead."[35] I'm sure that I, too, would have been horizontal, flat out on the ground, "as if I were dead."

Later in Revelation, John saw Jesus again. This time, though, Jesus was seated on a horse. Scripture declares His name to be Faithful and True. Once again, He had the same fire-eyes and the same sword coming from His mouth. He was coming to take His rightful place as King of all kings and Lord of all lords.[36] This depiction is apparently what the resurrected Christ looks like. Anyone who sees Him in such a form would have the same reaction as John: to fall down before Him. Compared with how we generally use the word, *worship* might almost seem too anemic a term. We don't generally react quite so strongly as we "worship," but that's exactly what we will do when we see Him as He is.

John's vision doesn't stop with the All-Powerful, coming-King picture. Just a few verses on down, we read these words: "Now the dwelling of God is with men, and he will live with them. They will be his people, and God himself will be with them and be their God. He will wipe every tear from their eyes. There will be no more death or mourning or crying or pain, for the old order of things has passed away."[37] Then, Jesus Himself adds, "I am making everything new.... I am the Alpha and the Omega, the Beginning and the End. To him who is thirsty I will give to drink without cost from the spring of the water of life."[38] What a great picture of the God who loves His people intensely!

The One Who created everything—the God of all—reached out in love to you and me. After we had turned away from Him, the Maker could have simply annihilated

His creation and started over, but He didn't. At the price of the life of His own Son, He ransomed us. Though it caused His own pain and suffering, He willingly laid down His life. What an incomparable and gracious God we serve.

The Lord is seen in Scripture as powerful and mighty, as well as kind and benevolent. Just like the old table prayer says, "God is great, and God is good." When we get the real picture of what God is like, based on His eternal Word—when we truly know His greatness and His goodness, not just how we'd like Him to be—our worship will become more in line with the worship of Heaven. To get to that point, we need to keep looking into His Word and see what He's really like.

GOING DEEPER

- If we tend to see and respond to God in terms of how He meets our expectations of Him, then who is really God in this situation? Explain your answer.
- In light of what we have been considering, when we give ourselves to the careful study of Scripture, what should be our main objective? (Look at Philippians 3:8-11 for guidance in this regard.)
- Rate yourself on a scale of 0 to 10 (0 meaning "not at all," and 10 meaning "as much as is humanly possible") on how diligently you give yourself to studying Scripture in order to soak in Who God is. What can you do to make this better?

We Do Not Reverence the Presence of the Lord

An acquaintance of mine told me he recently visited a church on Sunday morning. He said that during their twelve and a half minutes of "worship," many people went to the back to eat donuts and drink coffee. I couldn't help but be appalled. My reaction was immediate. What sort of leadership would allow—or, perhaps, even encourage—such a thing to occur? What does condoning such behavior say about our beliefs? They call this worship? I don't think so!

Some dear friends of our family are youth ministers

at their church. They welcome anyone into their youth services. Because there is a wide variety of young people who attend, during these gatherings, the leadership teaches everything, from basic Bible stories to what worship is. Many of the teens participate in worship near the front of the room, but others choose to stay in their seats. In the past, those in their seats would often sit and talk with one another, and not just in a whisper, either. My friends finally realized that by allowing this to happen, they were tolerating, as they put it, “an ungodly level of disrespect.” I think my friends got that one exactly right.

One of the distinctive characteristics of Christianity is that God is with us. Of course, we know that God is everywhere. The theological term is that He is omnipresent. Yet, the Lord has promised to always *be with us* and never to leave us (Deuteronomy 31:6, 8; Psalm 118:6-7). He dwells with His people. You won’t find a promise like that from Allah in the *Qur’an*. Only the God of the Judeo-Christian heritage has made such an audacious promise.

In the New Testament, though, Jesus took that concept to an entirely new level. He promised that “where two or three are gathered in my name, there am I among them” (Matthew 18:20). Something special happens when we gather in His name. The risen Christ comes into our midst. Exactly what that means and how it happens, I can’t answer. Honestly, no one on Earth can, with any degree of accuracy. It’s part of the mystery of God. All we know is that He’s there. Jesus didn’t give us the details, but we know He is trustworthy. So if He promised that He would be in our midst when we gather in His Name, then, truthfully, He is there. His presence is just as real as when Isaiah saw the Lord "high and lifted up" (Isaiah 6:1). Of course, we likely cannot actually see Him like Isaiah did, but He's there, just the same. He is every bit as real as we gather to worship Him. And whether we "feel it" or not is a moot point. Just like any other aspect of what we believe, it must be taken by faith. He promised, so we trust Him. He's there.

Many years ago, my sons and I used to play basketball out on our driveway. I was never much of a basketball player, so the competitions ended before they reached high school. What we did there on the driveway, though, didn't really compare with an NBA championship game. In fact, if you were to compare the two, you might even wonder if we were really playing the same game.

Similarly, a group of people gathering to hear some nice music and listen to someone talk doesn't really compare with a group of people who have honestly and wholeheartedly gathered in Jesus' Name to worship Him. If Jesus was serious when He said, "Where two or three are gathered in my name, there am I among them" (Matthew 18:20), then our actions should reflect the fact that He is present. Unfortunately, that's not usually the case. Too often we are far too casual, like the two churches I mentioned at the beginning of this chapter. We have lost the mystery of the risen Christ in our midst.

The place where we gather for worship—ancient cathedral, modern store front, or somewhere in between—

really has no specific spiritual connections. If we understand that Jesus did away with the idea of sacred and profane, with regard to locations, then meeting for worship in a building that is designated as a "church" is really no better than meeting in the back room of Denny's for worship. What *is* vital to recognize, however, is that *wherever* we meet becomes sacred because Christ is present. The King comes to be in our midst.

I've been told that the President of the United States has two Boeing 747s at his disposal. Both have a private office for the Commander-in-Chief. Both have special guidance systems, beyond the norm. Both are identical aircraft. Neither, though, is technically Air Force One. They're both just known by their individual call signs...until the President steps on board. Then, everything changes. Oh, nothing on the outside looks any different. The physical characteristics of that jet are still the same. But that aircraft suddenly becomes Air Force One. Why? Because of the presence of the President.

In like manner, when we gather in Jesus' Name, everything changes. It is no longer business as usual. The risen Christ is there in our midst. All the rules are altered. The ordinary becomes extraordinary; the natural becomes supernatural. Of course it does, because Jesus is there in a way that somehow transcends everyday life.

His being there in our midst truly is a mystery. If we ever think we have the Lord all figured out, we'll be wrong. Our finite minds cannot fully comprehend the Infinite. We just can't. How is Jesus in our midst as we gather in His Name? We don't know. It's a mystery. But our lack of comprehension doesn't make it any less of a reality.

Understanding that the Lord is indeed present in our service as we gather in His name causes our worship to take on a bit more of the characteristics of Heaven. Perhaps more to the point, it should cause us to distance ourselves from practices that would be foreign in Heaven. Could any of us honestly imagine that in the midst of the worship dramas depicted in Revelation there could be a group of people off on the side eating donuts and drinking coffee, watching the scene unfold? Could there be a group of people in the background of the scene sharing the latest gossip? Isn't the very idea ludicrous? So, why, then, would we allow—and, in some cases, even encourage—such things here and now? Tolerating such behavior sends a very wrong message to the participants. "It's okay to take God lightly." It isn't.

The twelfth chapter of Hebrews tells us, "Let us offer to God acceptable worship, with reverence and awe, for our God is a consuming fire" (Hebrews 12:28-29). That statement seems to imply that without reverence and awe, worship is not acceptable. That's a sobering thought. I'm not sure many people in our society today truly practice—or, perhaps, even understand—reverence. If the Lord is truly in our midst, then a flippant attitude seems grossly out of place.

You'll notice throughout this book that I've been reading a lot from A.W. Tozer lately. He can be harsh at times, but, from the perspective of many, he was one of the most notable voices of the twentieth century, endeavoring to keep the Church secured to its biblical moorings. Although he passed away almost fifty years ago, there is so much of what he said that reads as though he was speaking to people today. He frequently hits the nail on the head when it comes to the topic of worship. Tozer said this: "There is grief in my spirit when I go into the average church, for we have become a generation rapidly losing all sense of divine sacredness in our worship. Many whom we have raised in our churches no longer think in terms of reverence—which seems to indicate they doubt that God's presence is there."[39] If we truly believe that the Lord is in our midst—and we doggone well better believe it!—then how we act, what we say, and what we do are all of great importance.

If you were invited to Buckingham Palace to meet with the Queen of England, you might consider beforehand what would be proper behavior for such a meeting. Most assuredly, you would not walk into the room, stroll over to a nearby couch, plop your butt down, put your feet up, and say, "Yo, Queeny, wha'sup?" That is simply not the way one behaves in the presence of royalty. We know that. We recognize that there are proper ways of acting toward those who are, from an earthly perspective, our superiors. At work, we behave differently with the company owner or president than we do with the average coworker. We treat the guest speaker differently than we do our kids. If we were to have a meeting with our congressman, we would likely act differently toward him than if we were chumming around with some friends. These things are obvious to us. We don't need to spend a bunch of time figuring out such scenarios. So why do we so often throw all that out the window when we engage with the One Who is *supremely* higher than us?

Look again at those glimpses of worship from John's Revelation. His descriptions are detailed and breathtaking. He carefully recorded everything. You can bet that if John had seen the slightest hint of something going on that seemed out of place, we would have known about it. He would have told us. He would have seen it, written it down, and it would be right there for all of us to read. But there wasn't anything out of place. There was no flippant attitude, no "ho-hum, another worship service" way of thinking. There was, apparently, no slouching posture, no pretzel munching going on. People weren't conversing over on the side or checking the latest news updates or Facebook posts on their phones or tablets. Everyone there was in reverence of the Almighty God.

If He truly is in our midst as we gather in His Name, then that should be our attitude, also. I realize that we can't see Him, like the inhabitants of Heaven can. Yet, if we take Him at His Word, He really is there. He is present in a special way. Therefore, nothing else should matter. By comparison, everything else is mundane and trivial.

Before closing this chapter, let me add a few additional thoughts. Over the years, I have often referred to our relationship with God as primary. Relationship was, after all, the reason for creation. Jesus said it was the first and most important commandment. Relationship with the Lord should be at the forefront of all we do.

It should be understood, though, that there are two aspects to that relationship: *objective* and *experiential.* The objective is through faith in Christ's atoning sacrifice. Trusting in Jesus' death and resurrection puts us in right standing with God. That's the objective part of the relationship. The subjective, or experiential, is, just as the word implies, more of an experience. It can be like the old gospel song says, "He walks with me and He talks with me..."

A couple of centuries ago, Christian thinkers often referred to these two different aspects as *union* and *communion*. One is, in today's vernacular, a done deal. "See what kind of love the Father has given to us, that we should be called children of God; *and so we are*" (1 John 3:1, author's emphasis). By His grace, that relationship is sealed. The other aspect is the "walking out" of the relationship in everyday life. One is objective—once and for all complete; the other is subjective—an experience founded on the objective. One is union, the other communion.

Most people I have talked with through the years have said that the experiential aspect of the relationship grows and deepens as they intentionally draw near to God. This makes sense, since the Bible promises, "Draw near to God, and he will draw near to you" (James 4:8). As we make the effort to spend time in His Word and prayer, we sense His nearness. But such experiences are not automatic. It generally takes time and discipline on our part to draw near.

I say all that in this context, because it applies here. Recognizing that the Lord is present and actually experiencing that presence are two different things. As we gather in the name of the Lord, we trust that He is present, because His Word promises that He will be present. That's the objective part. At the same time, we should also be *experiencing* an increasing awareness that He *is* present.

Some time ago, I happened across a survey that indicated that the vast majority of regular church-goers do not sense the presence of God during their congregational gatherings. I think that's sad. But I would also suggest that it has implications on an individual level. If we are not intentionally drawing near to God in our relationships with Him on a personal level, then it is likely we won't know His presence in the larger group setting.

Of course, I recognize that in Heaven, we won't need to accept by faith that He is present. It will be clear and obvious. Here and now it's not the same. However, as we regularly spend time drawing near to Him through His Word and through prayer, we will experience Him more and more in the context of the corporate worship service. I would urge you, therefore, to take the time on your own—make the effort—to draw near to God. He will, then, draw near to you. You will experience Him more.

I encourage you, the next time you're involved in worship in a congregational setting, to consider what Heaven will be like with the true and real and living presence of God Almighty. In that setting, we won't need to prime the pump for worship. Instead, worship will pour out of us. It will be a natural and obvious response. Then, once you've pictured that scene, remember that just like the worship we see in Heaven, our God is present, and we can choose to worship Him.

GOING DEEPER

- How would your participation in worship at your church change if you chose to believe and count on the very presence of the Lord Jesus in your midst?
- What might you do to cultivate such a mindset in yourself? In others?
- Does how we regard worship at church really reveal how much or how little we really reverence the Lord Jesus Himself? Elaborate.
- Tom suggests that we take time to draw near to the Lord in the Word and prayer. What might happen if you laid aside all other agendas for your times reading and studying the Scriptures, and made the sole purpose developing your love relationship with the Lord, simply getting to know the One who loves you more than anyone else does?

Epilogue

In her book, *Praying with Authority*, Barbara Wentroble made an interesting statement.

> "In the Bible, God gives us pictures of what heaven looks like. He does not give us these pictures so that we will be homesick and always wanting to leave Earth and go to heaven. He gives us pictures of heaven so that we will know what he wants Earth to look like."[40]

I'm not sure that I *fully* agree with that statement.

According to Hebrews 11, there should be a longing for heaven here and now, a homesickness. At the same time, though, Wentroble has a point. Those heavenly glimpses help us to see the real pattern, one that we should be emulating here and now.

My goal in writing this book is to challenge and encourage all of us—leader and participant alike—to endeavor more and more to reflect the heavenly model of worship. Worship is not about liking or not liking certain styles of music or particular expressions. It is not about preferring a tradition of "this is the way we've always done it." It is certainly not about measuring how good you felt during or after the worship experience. True worship is about focusing your heart, mind, and strength on the Object of our worship, Almighty God.

Charles Spurgeon commented on Revelation 21:23, "The Lamb is the light thereof," by saying this:

> "Quietly contemplate the Lamb as the light of heaven. Light in Scripture is the emblem of joy. The *joy* of the saints in heaven is comprised in this: *Jesus* chose us, loved us, bought us, cleansed us, robed us, kept us, glorified us: we are here entirely through the Lord Jesus... Light is also the cause of *beauty*. Nought of beauty is left when light is gone. Without light, no radiance flashes from the sapphire, no peaceful ray proceedeth from the pearl; and thus all the beauty of the saints above comes from Jesus. As planets, they reflect the light of the Sun of Righteousness; they live as beams proceed-

> ing from the central orb. If He withdrew, they must die; if His glory were veiled, their glory must expire. Light is also the emblem of *knowledge*. In heaven our knowledge will be perfect, but the Lord Jesus Himself will be the fountain of it. Dark providences, never understood before, will then be clearly seen, and all that puzzles us now will become plain to us in the light of the Lamb. Oh! what unfoldings there will be and what glorifying of the God of love!... Whatever there may be of effulgent (brightly shining) splendour, Jesus shall be the centre and soul of it all. Oh! to be present and to see Him in His own light, the King of kings, and Lord of lords!"[41]

I don't know about you, but I'm looking forward to that day. Until that day, my goal is to more and more cause the worship of Earth to line up with the worship of Heaven.

Dr. David Jeremiah, pastor of Shadow Mountain Community Church in San Diego, California, believes that the "crescendo of praise and worship we are experiencing is in accord with His timeline because we are getting ever closer to the 'grand finale' of His purposes on earth, ultimately culminating with the praise of God in heaven."[42] We'll soon be home, free of all earthly hindrances to our worship. We'll get to experience—not just read about—true and complete worship, the way God intended it to be.

Bill Bright, founder of Campus Crusade for Christ, described it well in his book, *The Journey Home*. He gave this wonderful description of worship in Heaven:

> "Enthralled in the presence of the living Lord and Savior, we can expect to engage in the most glorious worship service of all time. No one has any sense of an "order of service." No one is conscious of any worship "style." The Father has set matters in order. The Son is the focus of all eyes. The Spirit prompts the singing of songs. From the lips of sinners saved by amazing grace come Hosannas to the King of kings and Lord of lords...."[43]

To the One who sits on the throne and to the Lamb be praise and honor and glory and power forever and ever. Amen!

GOING DEEPER

- Briefly list some of the main things that you have been learning while reading this book.
- Now, choose *one* thing that you believe you most want to follow up on, and describe in as much detail as possible *what* you want to do, *why* you want to do it, and *how* you are going to do it.

Notes

1. Revelation 4:8, NLT
2. Revelation 4:11, NLT
3. Revelation 5:2, MSG
4. Revelation 5:5, NIV
5. Revelation 5:9-10, ESV
6. Revelation 5:12, NLT
7. Revelation 5:13, NKJV
8. Revelation 7:10, NLT
9. Psalm 3:8, BBE
10. Acts 4:12, ESV

11. Revelation 7:12, ESV
12. see Revelation 22:18-19
13. http://talkwisdom.blogspot.com/2010/05/eternity-of-worship-in-heaven.html
14. I realize that some churches are not ethnically diverse simply because of the area in which they are located. Some friends of mine attend a church in a rural area. Within a ten mile radius, the population is ninety-five per cent white. As a result, their church is overwhelmingly white. That probably won't change anytime soon, simply because of demographics. However, a geographic area that is not at least somewhat ethnically/culturally diverse, especially in the U.S., is clearly becoming less and less the norm.
15. Greg Laurie, quoted by David M. Bailey in *Arrabon: Learning Reconciliation Through Community & Worship Music*, (Morrisville, N.C.: Lulu, Inc., 2011), pg 32.
16. David M. Bailey, *Arrabon: Learning Reconciliation Through Community & Worship Music*, (Morrisville, N.C.: Lulu, Inc., 2011), pg 32-33.
17. In fact, I would argue that if we're to be good stewards of all that we have, it includes our ear drums. Music that is too loud, will, over time, damage hearing. That's not an opinion; it is a scientifically and medically verifiable fact. We should be careful with volume in our church services. For a more complete treatment of this subject, read my article, "How Loud Is Too Loud?" at http://www.training-resources.org/loud_music.html
18. John Wesley's Rules for Singing, 1761, http://tobeapilgrim.wordpress.com/2007/10/05/john-wesleys-rules-for-singing-1761/
19. Stephen Altrogge, "Men, Let's Worship Like Real Men,"

The Blazing Center blog, http://www.theblazingcenter.com, 18 October 2012

20. Mark Altrogge, "What Does Your Worship Say About God" *The Blazing Center* blog, http://www.theblazingcenter.com, 19 October 2012

21. John Jefferson Davis, *Worship and the Reality of God,* (Downers Grove, Illinois: IVP Academic, 2010) pg 23

22. Chris Gambill, posted on Facebook, 11 May 2012

23. Dr. Robert Webber, "Let's Put *Worship* into the Worship Service," *Christianity Today*, February 17, 1984, pg 52.

24. C.S. Lewis, *Letters to Malcolm: Chiefly on Prayer*, (Orlando, FL: Harcourt, 1963) pg 4

25. Scott Wesley Brown, "Worship This Side of Heaven: The Call for Unified Worship," http://worship.com/2007/07/worship-this-side-of-heaven-the-call-for-unified-worship/

26. For a more complete understanding, see my book, *Becoming a True Worshiper*, where I develop the idea that biblical worship has three main components: it honors God, it is directed toward God, and there is an involvement on the part of the worshiper. Without all three of those aspects, what we do may be important and good, but, from an honest, biblical perspective, it isn't worship.

27. James MacDonald, "Unashamed Adoration," *Worship Leader* magazine, November/December 2012, pg. 21

28. Kim Gentes, "Why Worship Means Nothing," http://www.kimgentes.com/thinkjump-journal/2013/2/19/why-worship-means-nothing-thinkjump-journal-83-with-kim-gent.html

29.A.W. Tozer, *Tozer on Worship and Entertainment*, (Camp Hill, Penn.: WingsSpread Publishers, 1997) pg 115

30. Scott Wesley Brown, posted on Facebook, 20 January 2012

31. Glenn Packiam, posted on Facebook, 21 February 2011

32. A.W. Tozer, *Tozer on Worship and Entertainment*, (Camp Hill, Penn.: WingsSpread Publishers, 1997) pg 23
33. ibid, pg 67
34. Revelation 1:17-18, MSG
35. Revelation 1:17, NLT
36. see Revelation 19:11-16
37. Revelation 21:3-4, NIV
38. Revelation 21:5-6, NIV
39. A.W. Tozer, *Tozer on Worship and Entertainment*, (Camp Hill, Penn.: WingsSpread Publishers, 1997) pg 85
40. Barbara Wentroble, *Praying with Authority*, (Ventura, Calif.: Regal, 2003) pg 86
41. Charles Spurgeon, *Spurgeon's Morning and Evening Devotional*, August 3 AM
42. Dr. David Jeremiah, *Revealing the Mysteries of Heaven*, (San Diego, Calif.: Turning Point for God, 2009) pg 77
43. Bill Bright, *The Journey Home*, (Nashville, Tennessee: Thomas Nelson, 2003) pg 155

Final note: I intentionally used various translations of the Scriptures (a major departure from my normal writing and teaching) more because of copyright issues than anything else. Since the original scope of this project was to have a larger than usual percentage of the finished piece as direct quotations from the Bible, using too much from one translation could potentially be a copyright violation. So, even though the project evolved as I wrote, I opted to leave the various translations in place.

About the Author

Tom Kraeuter (pronounced Kroyter) is a Bible teacher, author, and worship leader. He serves as Executive Director of Training Resources, a ministry devoted to strengthening Christians in their relationships with God and with one another. Tom has ministered in hundreds of churches to tens of thousands of Christians. Tom's ministry is marked by his ability to apply Scripture to everyday situations.

Churches of all sizes have hosted Tom as a special guest and conference speaker. His most popular teachings are on worship and church unity. He has been welcomed by churches in nearly every state, from more than 40 denominations, including Baptist, Evangelical Free, Pentecostal, Lutheran, Presbyterian, Mennonite, and Vineyard.

Tom has attended Christian Outreach Church near St. Louis, Missouri, for more than thirty years. He and his wife Barbara have three adult children.

Contact Tom Kraeuter:

Training Resources, Inc.
65 Shepherds Way
Hillsboro MO 63050
636-789-4522
staff@training-resources.org

Check out our ministry websites

Training-Resources.org

WorshipSeminar.com

WorshipMinute.com

WorshipLeadingAnswers.com

WorshipMinistryDevotions.com

WorshipLeadingCoach.com

WorshipConferenceList.com

WorshipLeaderSummits.com

Other books by Tom Kraeuter

The Great Soviet Awakening
The True Story the West Was Never Told

Are There Terrorists in Your Church?

Worshiping God in the Hard Times

Reflecting God's Mercy in an Unmerciful World

Keys to Becoming an Effective Worship Leader

Oh, Grow Up!

Becoming a True Worshiper

The Worship Leader's Handbook

If Standing Together Is So Great,
Why Do We Keep Falling Apart?

Developing an Effective Worship Ministry

Times of Refreshing

Things They Didn't Teach Me in Worship Leading School

The Blessing of Obed-edom

Guiding Your Church Through a Worship Transition

Living Beyond the Ordinary

The Missing Element of Worship

More Things They Didn't Teach Me in Worship Leading School